Winning

The Design of Sports

Edited by Susan Andrew

With essays by
Patrick Burgoyne,
Dylan Jones,
Martin Pawley,
Richard Seymour,
Richard Williams and
Peter York

Laurence King
Publishing
in association with
Glasgow 1999

Winning

The Design
of Sports

The exhibition 'Winning' has received support
from The Scottish Sports Council, Nakagawa
Chemical Inc and Erco Lighting Limited

Published 1998 by Laurence King
Publishing, London
in association with Glasgow 1999
Festival Company Ltd
Laurence King Publishing is an imprint of
Calmann & King Ltd, 71 Great Russell Street
London WC1B 3BN
Tel: +44 171 831 6351; Fax: +44 171 831 8356
e-mail: enquiries@Calmann-King.co.uk

A catalogue record for this book is available
from the British Library.

ISBN 1 85669 152 7

Designed by Esterson Lackersteen
Picture research by Suzanne Hodgart

Printed in Italy

Contents

Contributors

Susan Andrew is a curator and writer. Formerly a curator at the Design Museum, London, she was responsible for numerous exhibitions including 'Frank Lloyd Wright in Chicago: the Early Years', 'Charlotte Perriand: Modernist Pioneer' and 'True Brit', a monograph of fashion designer Paul Smith. Her most recent project is the exhibition 'Winning: The Design of Sports' for Glasgow 1999 UK City of Architecture and Design.

Patrick Burgoyne is the Editor of *Creative Review*, the leading monthly magazine for the communication arts. He has written two books: *Bored: Surf/Skate/Snow Graphics* and *FC Football Graphics*.

Dylan Jones is the Editor-At-Large of *The Sunday Times Magazine*. He was previously Group Editor of Wagadon, publishers of *Arena Homme Plus*, *The Face*, *Arena*, *Frank* and *Deluxe*. Formerly a senior editor at *The Observer* and *The Sunday Times*, he has also worked for *The Independent*, *The Daily Telegraph* and *The Guardian* and was one of the first editors of *i-D*. He won the Magazine Editor of the Year Award in 1993 for his work on *Arena*. He is the author of six books on popular culture, including *Jim Morrison: Dark Star* and a portrait of the fashion designer Paul Smith, *True Brit*.

Martin Pawley is an architectural writer and critic who writes regular columns for *The Architects' Journal*, the Munich on-line magazine *Telepolis* and *World Architecture*, the magazine that he edited from 1992 to 1996. He is also UK architecture correspondent for the *Berliner Zeitung*. He has been architecture critic on *The Guardian* (1984–91) and *The Observer* (1992–95). He has written several books, most recently *Terminal Architecture*.

Richard Seymour is one of Europe's leading product designers. He formed Seymour Powell with Dick Powell in 1984, and the consultancy has clients as diverse as Nokia, British Rail, Yamaha, Tefal, Casio, MuZ and BMW. Richard has also worked in advertising, graphics, film production design and book design. He writes regularly in the British design press and has appeared on numerous TV and radio programmes, including the 'BBC Design Awards', 'The Late Show', 'BBC Design Classics', 'The Works', 'Woman's Hour' and Channel 4's 'Designs on your...' series.

Richard Williams was *The Guardian*'s sportswriter until 1997, when he became the paper's Film Critic. He joined *The Independent* in 1998. He has written several books including *The Death of Ayrton Senna* and *Racers*.

Peter York, an author, journalist and broadcaster, is a well-known commentator on lifestyle and social change. He writes on advertising for *The Independent* and contributes to a number of television programmes. In the 1980s he wrote the *Sloane Ranger Handbook* with Ann Barr. In 1996 he wrote and presented 'Peter York's Eighties', a six-part television series and accompanying book on social change in Britain for BBC2.

Introduction

The Sportification of Culture

Susan Andrew

'This is the Age of Sport... just as rock became the dominant cultural form of the 1960s and 1970s, so sport has become dominant in the 1990s, invading areas of life where previously it had no presence...' ('Worshipping the body at altar of sport', Martin Jacques, *The Observer*, 13 July 1997)

Sport is no longer mere sport: it is business, politics, art, film, TV, advertising, fashion, design. Certainly, sport is a global industry. In 1997 a study by the Georgia Institute of Technology calculated that in the United States, 'sport is a bigger industry than the motion picture, radio, television and educational services industries combined'. In the UK, the sports goods market was estimated to be worth £2,830 million in 1997; clothing accounts for 46.9 per cent of this sum, footwear 36.6 per cent and equipment 16.5 per cent. It is anticipated that this figure will continue to grow by an average of 5 per cent a year in the next three years. Sales of sports footwear have nearly doubled from £550 million in 1988 to £990 million ten years later, and trainers now account for 18 per cent of all shoe sales. As one Wall Street analyst said, 'Eisenhower used to warn of the military-industrial complex, now we have a media-athletic-shoe-company complex'. In 1997 the UK replica football kit industry was worth £200 million, with Manchester United clearly winning in the popularity stakes, selling around 850,000 shirts a year; in second place were Liverpool and Newcastle selling 600,000, followed by 500,000 for England. There are over 640 firms in the UK involved in motor sport engineering, producing an annual turnover of £1.3 billion, from the Formula One teams – in 1997 seven out of twelve were based in the UK – to makers of the other 3,000 car components. According to the Scottish Sports Council, hillwalking alone generates over £110 million.

In the 1990s sportswear is fashion. One review of the Autumn/Winter 1998 ready-to-wear shows in Paris exclaimed, 'Only the most flamboyant athletes need apply', as even John Galliano at Dior was moved to produce a 1920s floral take on parkas and puffa jackets. It is a widely held belief that sport has been the single greatest influence on everyday clothing since the French Revolution. Certainly most fashion innovations of

Left: Yohji Yamamoto, Spring/Summer 1997. Opposite: Tommy Hilfiger, Spring/Summer 1997. Following pages: Musto HPX Offshore suits use a combination of the latest fabric technology to create extremely tough foul weather gear.

recent years have arisen through developments in fabric technology, and the majority of these new fabrics are created by sportswear companies. Take fleece, the fashion success story of a 100 per cent polyester fabric that was first worn by explorers and mountaineers:

'Fleece: synthetic, unflattering, yet strangely irresistible...capable of conveying the sort of confounding message that has made fashion legends out of previous sportswear classics. The shellsuit made plasterers feel like leisured millionaires; argyle knitwear made pro-celeb golfers out of welders from Basildon...fleece hints that its wearer has just returned from the slopes at Mirabel.' ('Fleece', Judy Rumbold, *Observer Life*, 18 January 1998)

Enter 'spectator' wear: US research has found that fewer than one out of five sports shoes are actually worn for playing sports, with ranges from designers such as Donna Karan, Calvin Klein, Ralph Lauren's Polo Sport, and Tommy Hilfiger – who has also just linked up with Ferrari to provide clothing for the Formula One team and pit crew, and will add his

'sport is a bigger industry than the motion picture, radio, television and educational services industries combined'

red, white and blue logo to the new Formula One Ferrari.

A great design will not sell without the right promotion, and sport sells every kind of product, from chocolate bars and deodorant, to life assurance and cars. Manufacturers such as Adidas, Nike, Reebok and Puma recognize that they all produce good shoes, but acknowledge that people don't buy them because they have the best stitching. Athletes have endorsed and advertised products for decades, well before the boxer Henry Cooper, and more recently footballers Kevin Keegan and Paul Gascoigne urged us to 'Splash it (Brut) all over', or David Ginola's locks became the centre of attraction for L'Oreal shampoo. As can-do sports agent Jerry (Tom Cruise) says to his client Rod Tidewell (Cuba Gooding Jr) in *Jerry Maguire* (1996):

'I will not rest until I have you holding a Coke, wearing your own shoe, playing a Sega game featuring you, while singing your own song in a new commercial starring you, broadcast during the Superbowl, in a game that you are winning...'

In this instance reality eclipsed the plot: a product-placement deal had originally stipulated that the end credits of the film rolled over a Reebok ad, but the film-makers cut it at the last minute. In fashion advertising campaigns the 'heroin chic' look of recent years is now being traded in for an altogether more sporty, clean-living image, as in Calvin Klein's ads showing lightly tanned twenty-somethings enjoying hiking and walking. Meanwhile TAG Heuer, originally race timing specialists, have commissioned fashion photographer Herb Ritts to photograph some of the world's top athletes, including Wimbledon tennis champion Boris Becker, and 100-metre hurdler Jacqui Agyepong, to promote their new 'Kirium' sportswatch: the design brief had been 'to create a timepiece that looked as beautiful as the body of an athlete'.

Advertising and sport have never been as intimate as in the lead up to the world's biggest ever international sporting event, the 1998 World Cup. Stadia, players, balls and most of France became advertising space for the 12 'official' sponsors, including Coca-Cola and Adidas, who paid around £20 million each to appear on hoardings at all the games and to use the World Cup 98 logo on their

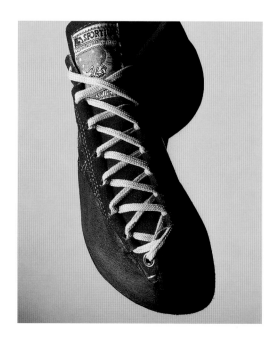

Previous pages: Using ladders to cross crevasses in the ice fall on Everest. Right: La Sportiva's 966 Mirage high-performance climbing shoe. Opposite: TAG Heuer's Kirium watch (1998). Following pages: Giancarlo Fisichella, one of the youngest Formula One drivers, with the components of a Formula One driver's outfit. All the clothing is made out of Nomex, a flame-retardant fibre introduced 25 years ago.

products. Nike, not one of the official sponsors, signed up the entire Brazilian football team on a ten-year contract rumoured to be worth $220 million; Adidas did a similar deal with the German team.

Sport is a passionate drama. Every Saturday sees scenes more gripping than Hollywood will ever manage, played out in the stadiums and arenas of the world, but that hasn't deterred athletes – more often in the United States than the UK – from trying to make the transition to the screen. Johnny Weismuller, swimmer and winner of five gold medals at the 1924 Paris Olympics, went on to portray Tarzan in 12 movies. While his protégé, the young Buster Crabbe, won the 400-metres freestyle at the 1932 Los Angeles Olympics and became Flash Gordon and Buck Rogers on the big screen. More recently, basketball star Michael Jordan appeared uneasily alongside a cast of cartoon characters in *Space Jam* (1996) and retired footballer Eric Cantona played the French Ambassador in *Elizabeth The First* (1998). It is not only on screen that an athlete can play a major role; when Daniel Day-Lewis was preparing for his role in Jim Sheridan's film *The Boxer* (1998) he underwent weeks of arduous training

from former world featherweight champion, Barry McGuigan. Perhaps the most successful example of sport on film is when athletes play themselves, as did Muhammad Ali – widely regarded as the greatest sporting icon of the twentieth century – in the Oscar-winning documentary *When We Were Kings* (1996). The combination of athlete, Hollywood star and sports fan is depicted in *He Got Game* (1998), a high-pressure week in the life of a high school senior basketball player, featuring the young real-life player Ray Allen of the Milwaukee Bucks, alongside Denzel Washington, and directed by an avid follower of the game, Spike Lee. Another regular spectator and basketball fan is film-maker Woody Allen, who has expressed the depth of his passion for sport:

'Basketball, or baseball, or any sport is as dearly important as life itself. After all, why is it such a big deal to work and love and strive and have children and then die and decompose into eternal nothingness?' (*New York Observer*, 25 May 1998)

Basketball is also an inspiration for American artist Jeff Koons who has

created numerous pieces inspired by the game, such as *One-Ball Total Equilibrium Tank (Spalding Dr. J. 241 Series)* (1985), which shows a mercury-filled basketball suspended in fluid, and *Encased* (1983–93): 30 basketballs and footballs packed in their logo-covered boxes and encased in glass cubby-holes. Koons says (with possible irony) that these pieces are the 'ultimate states of being for me'. Trainers often feature in the work of artists Jake and Dinos Chapman; their child mannequins, with genitalia for mouths and noses, wear nothing but Filas in *Zygotic exhilaration, bio-genetic, de-sublimated libidinal model (enlarged x 1,000)* (1995), recently shown in the 'Sensation' exhibition at the Royal Academy in London. Classical music is also experiencing a popular renaissance with a little help from football: in 1990 Luciano Pavarotti sang *Nessun Dorma*, chosen by the BBC as their World Cup theme, and classical music sales leapt by £20 million to £67 million overnight. For France 98 the BBC's title sequence was *Pavane* by Fauré which was packaged along with albums to mark the event, such as the Three Tenors singing their version of Queen's *We are the Champions*.

Above right: Interior of Nike Town, New York. Opposite: Jeff Koons, *Encased – Five Rows* (6 Spalding Scottie Pippen Basketballs, 6 Spalding Shaq Attaq Basketballs, 6 Wilson Supershot Basketballs, 6 Wilson Supershot Basketballs, 6 Franklin 6034 Soccerballs), 1983–93, 80" x 67$^1/_2$" x 17$^1/_2$"; glass, steel, basketballs, soccerballs.

Sport encourages the need for ever-changing up-dates in technology. Television has been used to produce some spectacular views of sport. During the 1998 Winter Olympics in Nagano the BBC provided the pictures of the bobsleigh and luge events for the rest of the world, and for the first time they buried three 'worm-cams' in the ice, which caught the bobs thundering and passing overhead to stunning effect. In Formula One motor racing, any one of the 50 billion audience can now get up close to their hero, thanks to in-car cameras.

Contemporary sport provides a stimulating brief for designers, although one commentator has dismissed sports design as part of

'the global conspiracy to swamp us in Day-Glo consumer goodies... [that] we don't need and only want because we feel we would look foolish or fogeyish without them. It is a very long way

'the global conspiracy to swamp us in Day-Glo consumer goodies ... [that] we don't need and only want because we feel we would look foolish or fogeyish without them'

from the design of a locomotive for a nationalized company.' (Jonathan Glancey, *The Guardian Space*, 29 May 1998)

Design is central to the development of sports, however – most sports equipment today has little in common with that designed 50, 20 or even 10 years ago. Many sports equipment and clothing companies are working with fabric manufacturers like Gore-Tex, ICI and DuPont to develop materials and technology to solve particular problems. Sports kit has become lighter and more comfortable and offers far more effective protection against the elements than was available 10 years ago. It was modern British-made marine clothing that helped to save the life of round-the-world sailor Tony Bullimore when his yacht capsized in the Southern Ocean in 1997. Nigel Musto, of Musto, one of three family-owned firms that dominate the British marine clothing industry, commented:

'If you fall into the water in two-piece gear in the Southern Ocean with temperature of 2 or 3 degrees you have about 15 minutes before you die of hypothermia. We asked skippers what would be a reasonable time period to pick a man up if they were ocean-racing and they said two hours. So we developed our one-piece suit which will keep you alive in the water for two hours.' (*The Guardian*, 6 January 1998)

Design and technology have also contributed to the dramatic reduction in fatalities in Formula One motor racing. Britain's first world motor-racing champion, Mike Hawthorn, used to wear a bow tie when driving, and Alberto Ascari, one of the greatest racing drivers of the 1950s, would drive in shirtsleeves and trousers. In the 1960s the wearing of flame-resistant overalls and helmets was made compulsory, and by the mid-1970s the governing body of motor racing introduced a standard for fire-resistant clothing and helmets that contributed to cutting fatalities down to two by the 1980s.

Design for sports also plays an increasing role in advancing human physical ability and makes it possible for more people to take greater risks. According to sports psychologist Matt Gough, 'in a hierarchy of needs, risk-taking sits right at the very top, with food and shelter at its base'.

Design for sports also plays a role in advancing human physical ability

Accordingly, once we achieve these basic needs we move up the scale to seek security, work, fulfilment through family, and finally we try to fulfil 'self-actualizing needs' – we test ourselves for its own sake. Commenting on Andy Green, who shot to global fame in 1998 as the fastest man on Earth after driving a British-built, jet-powered car at 1,150 kilometres per hour (714 mph) across the Nevada desert, Professor Cary Cooper, a psychologist at the University of Manchester's Institute of Science and Technology, states: 'It's not speed. It's the risk. That's what gives the buzz. And driving at 714 mph is certainly very risky.' Research suggests that more people are taking adventure holidays and escaping the nine-to-five routine by spending the weekends hang-gliding or rock-climbing. These 'weekend warriors' are showing an increasing interest in 'extreme' sports, such as street lugeing, base jumping, toe-in surfing, 'zorbing' (participants roll down hills in giant plastic balls), cave diving, or black-water rafting where rapids, ravines and waterfalls are negotiated on routes through underground caves. This interest seems to reinforce the idea that we crave an element of

danger in our lives. According to Frank Farudi, author of *Culture of Fear*, danger is actually good for us. Farudi considers that most of us are denied danger in today's risk-obsessed culture:

'Activities that were hitherto seen as healthy and fun – such as enjoying the sun – are now declared to be major health risks. Moreover, even activities that have been pursued precisely because they contain an element of danger are now reinterpreted from the perspective of safety consciousness. Pressure groups are demanding that new safety measures should be introduced in mountain climbing.'

Sport can be too risky, for spectators as well as participants, as the human disasters of Heysel and Hillsborough proved and which led to changes in the design of football stadia. One of the most recently built stadia is the £270 million Stade de France in Paris, designed by architect Macary Zublena Regembal Constantin. The world's largest multifunctional Olympic-sized stadium, it seats 85,000: a 'floating' roof covers all the stands, and there are 148 private boxes, 3 panoramic

148 private boxes, 3 panoramic restaurants, 43 cafés and snack bars, 2 giant 120 square metre (1,291 square foot) screens, 454 flood lights, 670 toilets, 17 shops, 36 lifts, and a pitch which cost £1,100 per square metre

Above right: British footballer Ian Wright, his vest showing a big Nike 'swoosh' and '179 Just Done It', having scored his 179th goal for Arsenal. Nike just did it again as the following day all the newspapers featured this picture. Opposite: Exterior view of the Stade de France in Paris (1998). Following pages: Land lugeing is just one of the 'extreme' sports created by those searching for more adventurous leisure activities.

restaurants, 43 cafés and snack bars, 2 giant 120 square metre (1,291 square foot) screens, 454 flood lights, 670 toilets, 17 shops, 36 lifts, and a pitch which cost £1,100 per square metre.

Women who take risks are a phenomenon that society generally views with disapproval. Alison Hargreaves, who died during her descent from the summit of K2, the world's second highest mountain, is a tragic example. Arguably Britain's best-ever female mountaineer, Hargreaves surpassed the achievements of many men when she reached the summit of Everest in May 1995 without oxygen or the help of Sherpas. Rather than focusing on her sporting achievements, however, people commented that she couldn't lead a proper family life because she left her children behind. Female boxing is another sport that has attracted disapproval. The first UK Women's Boxing Tournament was held in 1997 but world welterweight champion Jane Couch was refused a licence to fight. Headlines followed such as, 'Woman boxer is warned: Get hurt and sport may pay the price', and a doctor was quoted as saying, 'Boxing is a high-risk sport. Should such a tragedy occur when a woman is

boxing, the public adversity would put the whole sport at risk.' He added, 'in such circumstances it would be impossible to mount a medical defence of the sport'. Nevertheless, the British Medical Association is clear that it wants boxing totally banned: helmets can only protect against superficial injury, not brain damage.

Whatever the risks, sport has become increasingly popular with women. In the United States 40 million women participate in team sports: 7.2 million play soccer, and women's basketball draws TV audiences of over 2.5 million per week. According to the *New York Times*, women are taking more adventure vacations than men. The figures were certainly convincing enough for Condé Nast to launch the monthly magazine *Sports for Women* in 1997. The picture is not quite the same in the UK, where the Health Education Authority targeted their 1998 campaign 'Active for Life' at young women, research having found that only one-third of 16–24-year-old women are active enough to have positive health benefits, compared with over half of men the same age.

Design innovations have also enabled athletes to continue to break

records. In 1997 hinged klapp skates were introduced to speed skating, which led to ten world records being broken in the first three months of the season. At the 1998 Winter Olympics in Nagano it was silicone strips that caused controversy for the Dutch speed skating team. Experimental applications of these go-faster stripes to the back of their suits and helmets convinced the team that drag would be reduced, estimating that speed could be increased by half a second for each 400-metre lap. The result: the Dutch won gold, silver and bronze in the 5,000 metres and cut 8.5 seconds off the world record, its biggest improvement in 104 years.

There are many more examples of design innovations created by athletes and sports participants. In 1994 Scottish cyclist Graham Obree broke the World Hour record for the second time on a bike made with scrap metal and washing machine parts, but he was prevented from defending the title at the world championships as his bike was declared illegal. It was also Obree who introduced two revolutionary styles of riding, one where the arms are tucked in like a downhill skier and handlebars buried in the cyclist's

chest, and the 'Superman' riding position. The SpinGrip sole was conceived by retired executive Anthony Evans while sitting at his kitchen table one day. These soles were introduced on Umbro's football boots for the first time in 1998 and allow movement in a rotational direction, while still maintaining grip in a straight line. The SpinGrip is designed to reduce rotation injuries to knee and ankle – a major cause of incapacity to professional and amateur footballers alike.

As the margin between winning and losing becomes ever narrower and the human body is pushed to its physiological limits, design, new materials and technology are playing an increasing role in sports at all levels: extending the limits, contributing to the increasing numbers of people participating, assisting athletes to set new records and creating opportunities for new sports to develop. Whether it's in business, politics, art, film, TV, advertising, architecture, fashion, or design 'We are witnessing nothing less than the sportification of our culture.' ('Worshipping the body at altar of sport', Martin Jacques, *The Observer*, 13 July 1997.)

As the margin between winning and losing becomes ever narrower and the human body is pushed to its physiological limits, design, new materials and technology are playing an increasing role in sports

The Song of Pebax® on Kevlar®

Richard Seymour

Opposite: Nimble's Crosswind carbon fibre and epoxy composite bicycle wheel is the lightest wheel currently in production: a front wheel weighs 710 g. (25 oz.), a rear wheel 930 g. (33 oz.). On the rim is Vittoria's Professional All-Weather Tread. Below: (left to right) tennis rackets from 1830, 1910, 1930, 1976 and 1992, and the 1998 Head Ti racket. Ti rackets weigh 8 oz., 4 oz. less than the average racket. To get the racket this light, engineers made an extra stiff woven titanium and graphite frame and countered the resulting vibration with a dampener in the handle.

Where has all the romance gone? There used to be a time when a chap (or even a chap-ess, for that matter), could jolly well go out there and show his (or her) true mettle, with nothing more than a pair of canvas pumps on their feet, or a shagged-out catgut racket in their hand. One actually shuddered politely at the idea of using a technological advantage to defeat one's noble opponent, didn't one? Well, no...actually.

Dazzling though the array of smart materials, computer-analysed advantage factors and just plain sexy technologies there are out there nowadays is, technological cheating has always existed in sport, in one form or another. Sport is ritualized war. You win or you lose on the basis of your training, ability, fitness-level and technological firepower. But as in war, a psychological advantage is often as important as a real one. How often have you faced an unknown opponent on the other side of the court, clasping a glittering carbon confection and thought...'Jeez...I'm going to be slaughtered'? In the world of techno-enhanced sport/battle, it's often hard to differentiate between what is a legitimate technological improvement and what is a fake.

Several thousand years ago, the Assyrian cavalry picked up a handy technological advantage, which we now know as a 'composite bow'. But in those days, it was the Fist of God. Now, the Assyrians were pretty good at riding and shooting a bow at the same time (technique), and they were mean, meat-eating Mothers (training, fitness), but they also had a little twist on the bow-making technology. They found that if they made the limbs of the bow very stiff, usually with horn, and built the flexibility and springiness into the centre of the bow, using a laminate of wood and leather or sinew, it could drive a clothyard shaft clean through two soldiers at once (demonstrable technological advantage). Once demonstrated, word soon got around that the best place to be when an Assyrian bowman was in town was on another continent. The range and sheer violence of this new weapon struck abject fear into the hearts of the adversary...just like a Nike commercial does today.

Whether it's death by Assyrian or death by Lack of Street Cred, technology is the touchstone to the advantage...perceived or otherwise. Nowadays, no self-respecting sports equipment designer would be seen dead without a little acronym transfer

down the side of the product. Over the last 30 years, exotic technologies have become synonymous with sports equipment design. Football boots with precision polymers on the top surface, such as Craig Johnston's Adidas Predator Accelerator, combine smart materials with a sudden attack of common sense (let's stick a high-grip material, as found on a table-tennis bat, all over the kicking surface, rather than trying to skid-steer a wet ball!). Advanced fabrics that breathe as well as insulate, such as the long-established Gore-Tex, space-age spin-offs, such as Velcro and Kevlar (developed specifically for use in space suits and space vehicles), and PTFE with its very low surface friction, have penetrated not only sports equipment design but kitchen appliances as well in the form of Teflon coatings.

Some technologies enter sports and wither almost immediately as they cannot sustain their competitive advantage. Others, such as the introduction of Pebax and other injection-mouldable materials, into ski-bindings, come in and stay in as they totally eclipse the original material. For an entertaining afternoon in this area, it's hard to beat a visit to

the Museum of Tennis, in Wimbledon, where a historical cavalcade of 'things that worked and things that didn't' can be seen first hand. Aluminium rackets, double-strung rackets that put a savage spin on the ball (banned almost instantly), weird head designs and string layouts, weight-transfer rackets which use the theory of conservation of momentum to deliver a smashing blow at the peak of the serve: the whole thing is a salutary lesson in 'be good, but not too good, or you're a lousy cheat'. Head's latest proposal in this area is 'Titanium Tennis', a racket which weaves titanium (that super strong and light metal that fighter-jocks like to talk about a lot) and graphite to produce an ultra-light, wieldy result. They even provide a little window on the frame for you to view this exotic concoction.

One thing is for sure. Consumers expect technology to provide their edge in contemporary sporting activity. If the manufacturer is unable to deliver, then the consumer looks elsewhere. We have become a race of sporting technocenti.

When most people think of an example of a high-tech material nowadays, the words 'carbon' and 'fibre' tend to present themselves. Generally speaking, carbon fibre offers huge strength

and lightness when incorporated as a matrix into some form of resin or consolidating binder. Early adopters of this wonder material were the Formula One crowd, who rapidly appreciated its mouldability, strength, flexibility and lightness. McLaren's MP4 was the first to go the whole hog with a carbon-fibre monocoque body. Crash-cell and monocoque developments provided engineer and pilot alike with performance and, most important, safety. Anyone who's seen an F1 car pile unceremoniously into a pitwall with the energetic equivalent of an aircrash, and then watched the hapless driver stroll away from the conflagration with only his lipgloss smudged has had an object lesson in modern monocoque engineering brilliance.

Mike Burrows, father of the Lotus Superbike which took Chris Boardman to Olympic victory in 1992, is a carbon fibre enthusiast with a refreshingly bluff attitude to 'exotics'. When I met Mike at the Shimano European Bicycle Competition just after he'd rocketed to fame with his radical design, he mused over the way the media had latched on to the device itself: 'The bike was just what it should be, a relevant technical solution to a specific

Below: Therma-Pore™ 300 is a breathable inter-lining membrane: its non-woven polypropylene construction provides a wind-proof, breathable barrier that will repel wind-driven rain or snow, should the outer fabric become torn.

Left: Kevlar, Velcro and composites were originally developed in the 1950s for the US space programme which required light, strong and stable materials for space suits and vehicles. Opposite: The Adidas Equipment Predator Accelerator football boot, inspired by the surface of a table tennis bat, was conceived of by Craig Johnston, the ex-Liverpool player. He wanted a boot that increased a player's contact, control, grip and stability.

series of problems. Early experiments in carbon fibre on bicycles just replaced the steel with carbon, and that was completely the wrong thing to do. It saved weight, certainly, but it created problems of its own. Carbon fibre is not steel, and it performs in an entirely different way, but it was the way the bike looked that really captured people's imagination.'

Mike's design provided an aerodynamic blade, a monocoque, which took the loads and input energies of the cyclist and diverted them to where they were needed, in propelling the device forward at the maximum rate. Moreover, the form of the thing was transformed into a glittering, lacquered arachnid, crouching on the line next to objects that had remained virtually unchanged since the 1880s. The media went nuts (naturally, considering the result), and a galvanic jolt passed through the world of cycling. Suddenly, conventional tubular structures were hopelessly old hat, and manufacturers like Trek and Cannondale went on the warpath, producing carbon, aluminium and boron products which broke up the conventional outline of the bicycle and brought a new wave of tricked-up products directly to the waiting masses. Modern, fully-suspended

mountainbikes, available in any cycle shop, now rule the roost as far as street, and mud, cred are concerned. The weirder the shape, the tech-ier the rear suspension assembly looks, the happier the customer is. At the top end of the market, K2 has launched a fully suspended bike which possesses a 'smart shock', a piezoelectric spring which stiffens up under load (stolen from an F-18 fighter tail stabilizer, apparently).

But have you watched the Tour de France recently on TV? Where are all the weird shapes? Where are the exotic solutions? The fact is that most of the bikes you will see honking up the slopes look eerily like the original Rover patents of the end of the last century. They are actually oozing with state-of-the-art bits, but the

structure is the good old Peterson 'double triangle'. The image of the bicycle has, to an extent, leaped ahead of its practical, manufacturable function, with customer expectation driving the form to greater diversity. But that is what we want: technological credibility, sometimes at any price.

The great thing about bicycles, though, is that they're relatively simple devices. Anyone can afford to buy the top gear without selling their house. Porsche's latest high-speed lip-smacker isn't a rear-engined sports car, but a mountainbike of exquisite beauty and purpose. At £3,000 it's hardly a snip, but it is the two-wheel equivalent of a Le Mans racer. The forks are of such large diameter that they seem to have

Previous pages: Cyclist Chris Boardman on the record-breaking Lotus Superbike designed by Mike Burrows. Left: The Porsche Bike FS, 1997. Below: Trek's Y Foil 66. Bottom: Amber Tintsman in the Women's Downhill at Big Bear Lake , California (1997).

come directly from the front end of a trials motorcycle. Anodized adjusters and glittering alloy machinings wink from every crevice. There's one sitting in the window of Porsche Design's shop just off Rodeo Drive in LA, whispering come-hither encouragements to the credit-card *nouveau riche.*

How many of these things will end up screwed to the wall of fashionable loft apartments, rather than hurtling down the grit-slopes, one can only imagine, but this phenomenon needs careful scrutiny. Nike, when they started out on their long road towards global domination of the sports footwear market, coined an interesting term: Athleisure. What this meant was that people bought things for ordinary, everyday use that suggested that they were not sofa-bound invertebrates, but were in fact covert sportsmen in mufti. Now this is hardly a surprise, especially when one analyses Nike's entire marketing strategy, but a cynic would look at this whole thing and say that we are all being horribly manipulated. I admit I own a Ducati 916 myself, still one of the most desirable pieces of kinetic sculpture on two wheels, yet I couldn't possibly begin to approach the level of skill necessary to use it properly in

anger. I own it because it goes like stink, it looks beautiful and it makes me feel more capable than I actually am. Granted, being 19 stone, I guess I don't fool anybody anyway. But this sense of owning 'the best' is a powerful, primeval urge which subverts the wallet in a sinister manner. If I wear the right battledress then maybe some of the skill will percolate through...pathetic, isn't it? Yet I guess we all do it to some extent. And the manufacturers know this. And so do the designers. Seymour Powell recently produced a new computer-game joystick for the Hong Kong-based company Saitek, which had to balance these factors very carefully. The stick itself is extremely advanced, with lots of precision parts and trick software, yet this is no longer enough in the new sports frontier of digital combat; the device has to look the part as well.

There is a dilemma here for the designer. Do they shamelessly style-up the object to appeal viscerally to the user, without bringing genuine new benefits? Or do they go the Burrows route and try to improve the breed and hopefully achieve a trick new look in the process? A study of Olympic precision target-shooting devices yielded the right direction eventually. The biggest problems

with most joysticks is that they don't fit anybody perfectly. Normally, the idealized grip-moulding is based on some nebulous ergonomic norm which means that, over hours of slaying zombies, players get repetitive strain injuries if they're not careful. Seymour Powell's new controller has a fully adjustable grip, key head and trigger angle set-up which means that players can tune the object for perfect control. The resultant look is, to say the least, menacing. All the ergonomic adjusters and pads make the object appear like The Jackal has taken up *Resident Evil.*

Now, I can live with this, because the device is a genuine improvement. What you see is what you get. But how does the consumer ever really know whether they're getting a genuine advantage...or just snake oil? Easy – real-life performance. Sampras is kicking ass with his new racket, and Mr Jordan is surely smiting the sinners due to his superior footwear. Anyone who follows Formula One racing is struck by this conundrum all the time: is it the machine or is it the man? The great thing about Formula One is that if anyone actually picks up a significant advantage through technology then a) that idea will rapidly be adopted by the competition or b)

Trek's Y Foil 77 carbon-fibre frame one-piece road bike weighs just 19.5 lb. (8.9 kg.).

it will be banned next season. The powers that regulate the sport are deeply concerned that people continue to watch it, otherwise the powers won't be fabulously rich any more. And the domination of one team (as opposed to one driver) is considered to be, eventually, bad for the sport. A sort of Geneva convention for motorsport. We love the idea of a man, or woman, being so God-given omnicompetent that they tower above the rest (Michael Schumacher etc.), but we can't handle this technical 'cheating' issue, can we?

Fortunately, things continue to move forward. Every season, someone has some new tune to play on aerodynamics or combustion or transmission which gives a new wrinkle to which team dominates. But where do all the technical innovations go which are wrought in the heat of combat? Does Formula One create anything useful for the rest of us? Well, yes, actually. Many of the early active suspension ideas came from racing, not to mention sophisticated aerodynamic control, electronic engine management and combustion development. Push-button gearshifting and advanced energy-absorbency issues (safety, to you and me) have been stimulated also. If you don't have a handy war around, then multi-billion dollar sporting circuits often do just as well at creating new technologies and ideas. At the white-hot tip of technological development, hype doesn't get you very far....

Regardless of the hype, the sports footwear market is still the closest most of us are going to get to real technology-driven high-street product. Adidas, the German-based *bête noire* of Nike, really does put its money where its feet are. At the main design facility in Herzogenaurach, a team of specialists work full-time on developing material properties which will give significant performance edges to its products. Even cynics like me are staggered at the science that is actually applied to the development of objects which will, by and large, be worn by overweight wannabes whilst mowing the lawn. Adidas's main marketing platform, pitched against Nike's AIR approach, is the concept of Feet you Wear, an irrefutably sensible proposition, which suggests that the human foot is actually good at doing what it does all on its own, and that almost any extra stuff loaded on to it actually reduces the efficiency of the foot. The objective is to create as little hindrance to the movement and efficiency of the foot as possible whilst providing good control, shock reduction and support, not to mention protection against sharp things. Adidas has created some pretty interesting solutions to this conundrum in the past, by combining materials that soak up shock like a sponge and those that bounce back like a Superball. On a recent visit to the factory, I had the good fortune to have a lot of this demonstrated first hand by Mikael Pevito, resident distance runner and shoe designer. Assuming the position that Galileo must have taken at the top of the Tower of Pisa, he drops two identical balls of elastomer on to the hard factory floor. One rebounds like Buzz Aldrin and the other stops dead on the deck, absorbing every erg of rebound energy. 'We put the dead guy on the heel strike area, so that the impact shock is reduced', explains Pevito, 'and the bouncy one under the metatarsal heads and big toe, so that the launch is as frisky as possible....' In between these two active areas, the factory sticks a speculum-shaped semi-rigid stabilizer which helps control the shoe as the foot rolls through its normal movement cycle. As well as this 'body machine', tracking the foot's movement and

Right: Joystick for computer games peripheral manufacturer, Saitek. Opposite: Richard Seymour with his Ducati 916.

supplying complementary activity where required, the rest of the shoe bristles with extra smarts: conforming prosthetics that form to the underside of the foot, breathable materials which track away the whiff, not to mention a nickelodeon of flash styling materials on the outside, intended to attract the attention of the passing Olympian.

And this is where things start to get a little problematic. State-of-the-art running shoes do not illustrate the dictum 'form follows function'. Sure, they're jam-packed with techno-goodies, but there is a strong feeling within Adidas that the product forms should express the functional benefits in a vivid and exciting manner (they do have to sell to groovy young things, after all). What this leads to, in my personal opinion, is a very tenuous link between the benefits and full-on postmodern zaniness, and the definite risk that the technical message is lost in the product presentation. But does this matter? Well, to me it does, because it diminishes the strongly technical (or authentic) message that Adidas could be promoting. If technical performance is what you're standing for...?

What this vividly demonstrates is the eternal tension that lies between authenticity and marketability. The competition Olympic bow, with its balance weights and spider-like posture, is the ultimate expression of formal obedience, and because of this it's really exciting to look at as well. It's like that because it works like that and there is very little room for superfluous gewgaws. Indeed, just like the original Assyrian bow, with its fat centre section and heavily recurved limbs, it is this differentiation between the run-of-the-mill and the full-on combat version that makes the user and viewer salivate (or defecate, depending on the occasion).

So what does this all mean at the end of the day? Basically, designers are often the last people that technologists approach when it comes to the commercial exploitation of new materials. I can't remember the last time that a company approached me with a new material or manufacturing technique and said: 'What do you think you could do with that?', yet surely the designer is the first person they should approach, as the wide 'bandwidth' of the designer can often see beyond the mere mundane technical application of the material and imagine the exciting, unexpected

applications. Even the best examples of integrated design and technology, such as Adidas's own materials skunkworks, still find themselves seeking out the materials rather than having materials thrust upon them. Someone once said that the laser was a 'solution looking for a problem', as it existed theoretically, and even actually, decades before the applications of its extraordinarily coherent light began to emerge. It sat around in weapons labs and on geeky engineering benches until people with existing problems began to become aware of its benefits and fitted them to their own requirements. Holography was only a theory until someone stumbled on the laser to make it all work...but the theory goes back to the beginning of the century. We need a system where the technology can meet the application. Where materials manufacturers can propagate their ideas directly to the very people who can apply the necessary imagination to utilize their properties. This not only goes for sports equipment, it goes for everything. If you've got some trick new technology hanging around, don't just wait for the world to come to you. Give me a call.

A bronze medal winner at the 1996 Paralympic Games, Todd Schaffhauser runs on the Endolite 160 Hi-Activity prosthetic leg designed and manufactured by Blatchford. Athletic performance prostheses use materials such as carbon fibre, graphite and silicon.

Left: Men's Giant Slalom racer Jurgen Egle at the 1998 Winter Paralympics in Nagano. Opposite: British Archer Gary Hardings with a competition Olympic bow.

2 Image is Everything

Patrick Burgoyne

Opposite: The Brazil football shirt of 1997, worn by Ronaldo. Following pages: Glasgow Rangers football shirt with McEwans lager and Nike branding, and Celtic football shirt with Umbro branding.

Imagine a tennis court with no lines on it. Or a football pitch with no penalty areas being played on by two teams wearing exactly the same clothing. At a very basic level, graphics are an integral part of sport. Shirts featuring simple, bold graphic devices allow for the speedy, essential identification of team-mates. Names and numbers aid the process further, and geometric systems of lines and circles delineate playing areas. But graphics have a wider, perhaps greater importance in the world of modern professional sport. It is still possible to play football or rugby without matching shirts with squad numbers and players' names on the back, as hundreds of scratch games in parks all over the world everyday confirm, but what would be missing is the ritualized identification of and with the team which makes professional sport so compelling and so successful.

Professional sport could not exist without fans willing to pay to see their heroes. The sports that pull in the greatest number of paying fans are the ones that exploit the tribal instinct to the full: rugby, baseball, basketball, football and its American namesake. Affinity with a particular team is forged by its adoption of a distinct identity, usually involving a badge or logo and a distinct set of colours arranged in a set pattern that, in essence, rarely changes. The roots of such identities can be traced back to nineteenth-century regimental and school uniforms, when most modern sport was codified and popularized, although it can even be traced back to heraldry, where opposing teams and opposing fans come together under their colours as armies did in previous centuries.

This identification by colour is stronger in some sports than others. It is possibly at its strongest in football, where Manchester United fans sing 'Come on you reds' and Manchester City fans 'Blue Moon', and at its weakest in cricket where both sides once wore white. But even here colour plays a part in identification – on caps and sweaters. And it is worth noting that when the game's administrators sought to rid the game of its stuffy image and attract more spectators, among the first things they did was to introduce coloured clothing, to less than universal acclaim.

Not just any colour works. Traditionally bold, primary colours with their connotations of strength and vigour were favoured. Not many teams in any sport would consider playing in pink or brown (with the exception of a brief period in the 1970s when Coventry City somewhat shamefacedly turned out in a chocolate brown away strip), but palettes do vary from sport to sport. Football may favour red and blue above anything else, but Rugby Union with its links to public school has always been a little more adventurous: London's Harlequins club include the aforementioned pink and brown in their multi-hued jersey. In horse racing, where the colours of a jockey's silks are those chosen by his mount's owner, no shade is too garish and no combination is left untried. Diamonds, circles, and even stylized elements from traditional military dress uniforms are used. The insatiable desire of American football to generate the maximum spectacle has led to teams wearing striking colour combinations, such as the black and metallic silver of the Oakland Raiders.

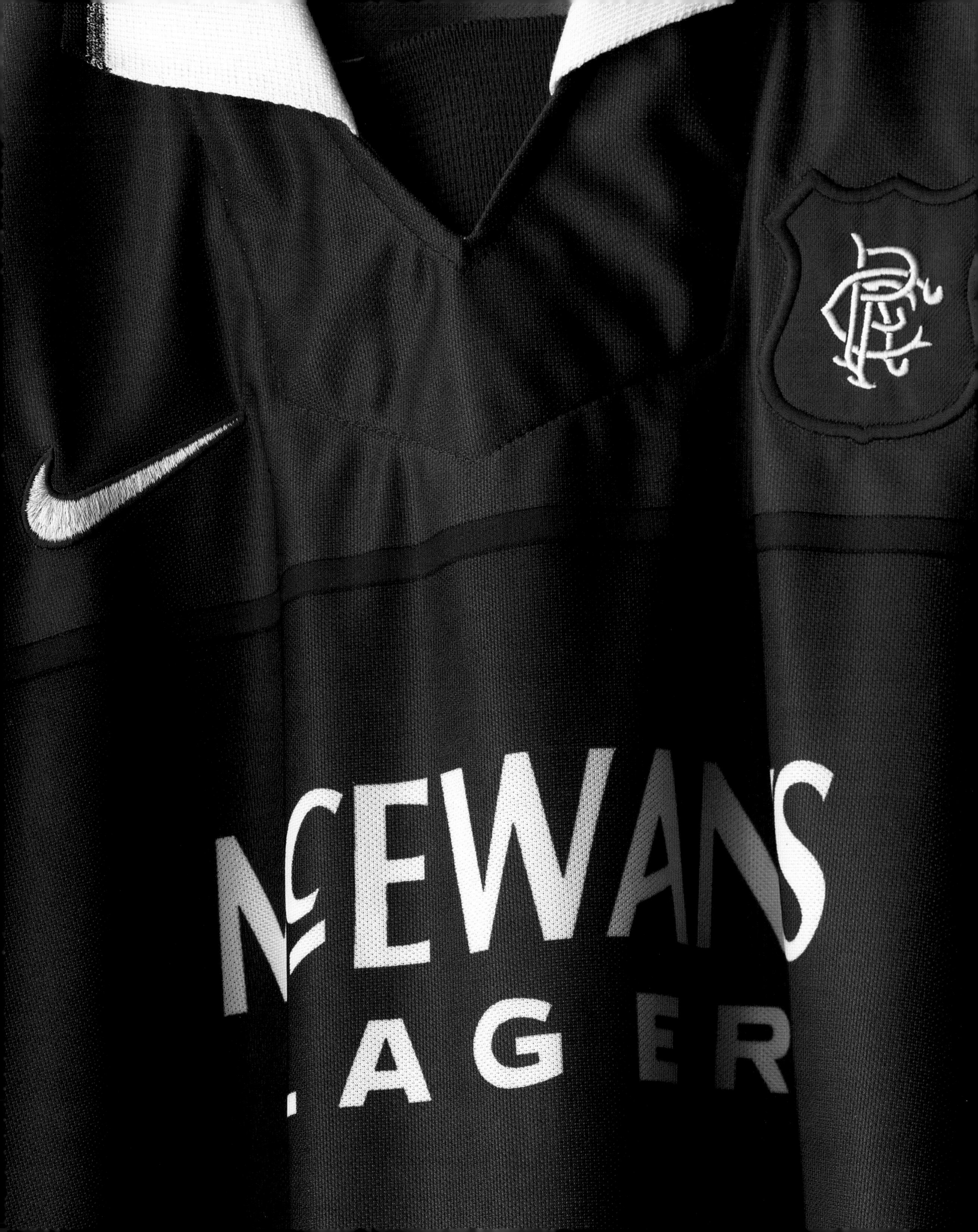
McEWANS
LAGER

Opposite: Football
fans display
team loyalty and
membership of the
'tribe' in all sorts of
ways, from wearing
the team shirt to
painting their
faces with the team
colours. Below:
Stripes, hoops and
quarters are the
recognized graphic
symbols of football.

As well as accentuating the tribalism that has created the phenomenon of the 'supporter', graphics have also played a central role in forming the distinct visual languages which many sports have created. Think of the iconic role of the yellow jersey or *Maillot Jaune* worn by the race leader in the Tour de France, or, to a lesser extent, the red-and-white polka dots worn by the King of the Mountains in the same event.

But polka dots would never be worn by a rugby team. Indeed, rugby teams virtually never wear vertical stripes and are far more likely to incorporate more than two colours in a shirt than, say, a football team. And just as certain hues are football colours, for example, so are certain graphic styles. Stripes, hoops and, to a lesser extent, quarters are football styles, whereas chevrons, spots and squares are not.

Individual sports have acquired their own specific iconography, their own graphic languages which are identifiable and promote a sense of belonging to their followers in the same way that successful brands create loyalty among consumers. London-based design group Tutsells@The Brand Union conducted a study into international football shirts as if they were looking at the packaging for a soap powder. They looked at such criteria as a shirt's visibility on screen, the relevance of its design, its distinctiveness and the extent to which the country concerned 'owned' the colours used. On this basis, Tutsells concluded that the two most successful team shirts were Brazil and Holland – not a bad correlation with the genuine balance of power in international football.

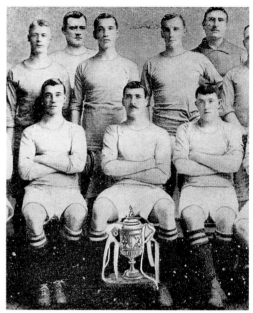

David Pearman, one of the designers who conducted the exercise, claims lessons can be drawn from football for other areas of marketing. 'Owning a colour is particularly relevant,' he says. 'You can go to a game and immediately you know who is supporting who. Brands such as Cadbury, with its use of purple, realize the importance of owning a colour in terms of aiding recognition. If you are consistent and bold you can build up an identifying relationship that makes it easier to sell your brand.'

The visual language of sport is frequently used as source material for creating identities in other fields. This is happening particularly in football at the moment, but other sports have been similarly plundered. The images of hot-rodding and motocross have long been popular in fashion and have been re-worked by graphic designers and typographers.

Above: In 1904 the
Manchester City
football kit looked
very plain compared
to the sponsor-
emblazoned kits of
today, the sales of
which represent a
huge income for
clubs. Following
pages: Sponsors' logos
are part of a football
team's identity.
Page 52: (from top
left) Flamenco
(Brazil), Nigeria,
Penarol (Uruguay),
Ajax (Holland), Inter
Milan (Italy), Necaxa
(Mexico). Page 53:
Croatia.

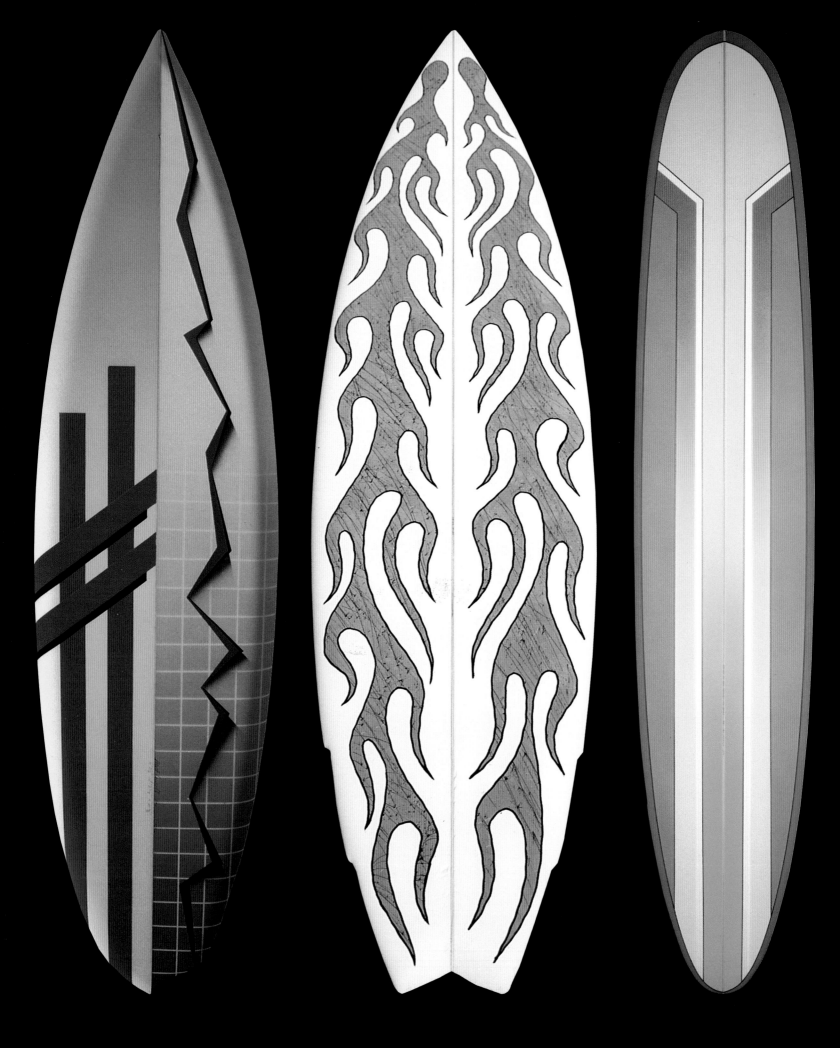

Previous pages: In the Tour de France the iconic yellow jersey, or *Maillot Jaune*, is worn by the race leader, while the King of the Mountains wears red-and-white polka dots. Opposite and below: Surfboard graphics (1985–91) by Californian artist Matt Micuda; airbrush, fluoro. Following pages: Skateboard graphics by Fuct. The company sets out to produce controversial, sometimes sexually explicit, graphics.

But no sports have enjoyed such a long and close relationship with the fashion and graphic design industries as the surf/skate/snowboarding scene. No other sports give graphics such a central role. Matt Micuda, who has been designing graphics for surfboards for 15 years, maintains that his customers buy a board simply for its graphics and not for how it performs. In skateboarding this is even more extreme. Most boards are made in exactly the same way, using exactly the same materials. The only distinguishing factor is the illustration on the board's base. (This is doubly ironic as the graphics start to be scratched off the moment that the board is used and are often obliterated by customized stickers as the owner personalizes his or her 'deck'.) Skateboard graphics express the rebellious, hedonistic culture which has become identified with the sport and which has made it so attractive to kids. 'If it demands confrontation, then it's a good graphic,' says Erik Brunetti, owner of skateboard company Fuct, in *Bored: Surf/Skate/Snow Graphics*. Boards feature any subject matter that might be popular at the time – bands, cartoons, brands, film stars – but with that certain twist of skate attitude. The full gamut of graphic and illustrative styles is used from psychedelia through to manga and David Carsonesque distressed typography.

Aaron Betsky, curator of architecture and design at the Museum of Modern Art in San Francisco, explains that the value of the board sports' aesthetic is as 'a vehicle through which the world of the street becomes honed down by its audience and translated into a selling tool by a wider graphic community. It has acted as a funnel for what is going on in street culture so that it feeds back into the commercial world of design and advertising.'

In turn the design community has sought to work in the board sports area because of the freedom and the credibility that it offers. Many design companies seek out snowboard companies as clients because they are willing to take risks and because they see boards and the associated catalogues as a highly visible medium for their work. Robynne Raye, a partner in Seattle design company Modern Dog which works for snowboard company K2, has described working in the industry as 'a designer's dream job'.

In terms of contributing to the creation of actual equipment used, other sports do not offer quite such opportunities. Most sporting footwear, for instance, is designed in-house by specialists rather than using outside consultancies, as are the graphics on clothing. However, sporting organizations and sports-related companies currently make up some of the most desirable clients in the creative industries. This is a result of the increased sponsorship and marketing opportunities growing up around sport which have led not just to the big budget Nike commercials which now dominate our TV screens, but also to sports themselves becoming more alive to the benefits of promotion: no sporting event of consequence would be complete, for example, without a graphic logo and mascot. This has reached its apotheosis with the Olympic games.

The 1932 games in Los Angeles were the first to have an official logo but it was not until the 1950s that the logo became an integral part of both bidding for and hosting the event. Both Summer and Winter games

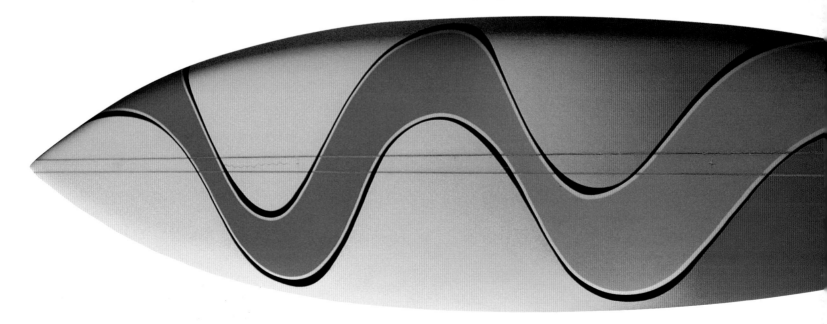

Sydney 2000

Opposite: Cobi, the cute mascot created by Spanish graphic designer Javier Mariscal for the 1992 Barcelona Olympics. Above: The Olympic logo for Sydney 2000, designed by Michael Bryce.

Above: A real dog called Smoky was the first – unofficial – Olympic mascot at the LA games in 1932. Right: Sydney 2000's three mascots, Olly, Syd and Milly, created by designer and illustrator Matthew Hatton. Following pages: Olympic games posters.

have thrown up sometimes striking, at times bizarre and often condescendingly kitsch imagery in an attempt to marry the Olympic ideal with a geographical location. Some organizing committees choose obvious symbols of their cities or countries, such as the stylized Stalin-era 'wedding cake' skyscraper that appeared as the logo for Moscow 1980, or the red sun of Tokyo 1964. Logos for the Winter games are dominated by snowflakes with various approaches taken for Grenoble 1968, Sapporo 1972, Sarajevo 1984 and Calgary 1988. One of the more adventurous logos was that produced for the 1960 Winter games held in Squaw Valley, USA which features geometric shapes in blue, yellow and red. And of course, appearing in all these designs is one of the most familiar logos of all time, the Olympic rings.

For Sydney 2000, the organizing committee has plumped for what it calls the Millennial Athlete. This is an abstracted, leaping figure designed by Michael Bryce which, according to the organizers, alludes to boomerangs, sun, rocks, beaches and the continent's red interior. Above its head, a wavy blue line is intended to recall the architecture of the Sydney Opera House.

Investing such marks with so much meaning can be a little tricky to sustain – without the above explanation it is doubtful whether even the most design literate would spot such a panoply of references in the Millennial Athlete – but this is the way such events work. They are routinely billed as celebrations of humanity and all that is good and their identities must convey that. And if the resulting logos can be somewhat bizarre, check out the mascots.

For, as each Olympics must have a logo, so must it have some kind of, preferably cute, sometimes cuddly, little critter with which to give the huge money-making extravaganza a friendly face. The first, unofficial, mascot was a real dog, Smoky, who appeared at the LA games in 1932 (with both the first logo and mascot, LA was way ahead of the field in its marketing of the event). Since Smoky, however, mascots have tended toward the illustrated rather than the animated. We have had Waldi, a rainbow-coloured dachshund from Munich 1972, Misha, the 'friendly' Russian bear from Moscow 1980 and Vuchko the wolf from Sarajevo 1984, but the award for excess cutesiness has to go to Heidi and Howdy. These two hideously saccharine white bears wearing stetsons were best avoided at the Calgary Winter games of 1988. For Sydney, we have not one mascot but three: Olly (a kookaburra), Syd (a platypus) and Milly (an Echidna – a kind of spiny mammal). The organizing committee's general manager for marketing, John Moore, has said of his furry friends 'what people wanted was something uniquely Australian, that really personified what Australia and Australians are all about'. The three characters were chosen from hundreds of submissions from around the world but Australian designer and illustrator Matthew Hatton's drawing of a platypus was the committee's favourite and led to him being appointed head of the mascot design project. Such selection procedures are common practice – one such competition resulted in the adoption of probably the only Olympic mascot of any enduring interest or merit, Cobi.

TOKYO 1964

OLYMPIAD 80
MOSCOU MOSCOW MOCKBA

XIVèmes jeux olympiques d'hiver
Sarajevo 1984

Yougoslavie

XIV Olympic Winter Games
Sarajevo 1984

Yugoslavia

XIV zimske olimpijske igre
Sarajevo 1984

Jugoslavija

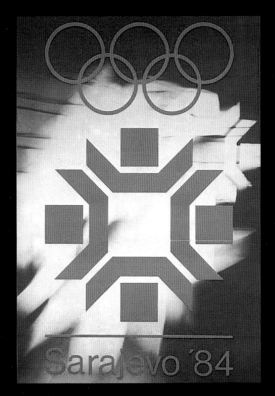

Sarajevo '84

Spanish graphic designer Javier Mariscal entered the contest to create a mascot for the 1992 games in his home city of Barcelona with what he has described as 'the son of a Catalan sheepdog and an unknown mother'. His cute little dog was designed to fulfil four functions: arousing sentiment, versatility, representing the city of Barcelona and acting as a host. After winning the contest, Cobi was first used by the Barcelona organizing committee in 1988. Dressed variously as a journalist, a fireman, a doctor and so on, he adorned even official communications. Mariscal developed his character by creating comic books, cartoons and even making a record so that, by 1992, over 1,000 items of merchandise featuring Cobi and his furry form appeared all over the city in both 2-D and 3-D guises. Mariscal has attributed Cobi's success to the fact that he was 'affable and modest, a naked puppy with no lessons to teach, only good humour and friendship'. That such qualities can be attributed to such an enormous, commercially aware, politically complex event as the Olympic games is testament indeed to the power of graphics in sports marketing.

The ever-increasing role of sponsors in the marketing mix, whether involved with individuals or teams, makes graphics even more important in modern professional sport. In motor sport, for instance, a sponsor's graphics are often inextricably bound up with the identity of a team. The McLaren Formula One car became famous for its red and white livery not because those colours say 'McLaren' but because they say 'Marlboro'.

And when a company is paying a player hundreds of thousands of pounds to endorse its equipment, it needs to be instantly obvious to the viewing public which brand it is that is gracing the feet, or racket or bat of their heroes. Manufacturers can tantalize consumers with the possibility of being able to buy the same kind of equipment that they have seen their heroes using.

Every item of kit used and worn by a professional sportsperson is now branded to within an inch of its life. The best graphics are simple, bold and can be recognized at a distance so that potential customers know which brand is in use: Gray Nicolls cricket bats, for example, use a thick red stripe on front and back, and Wilson tennis rackets feature a giant 'W' stencilled on to the strings.

In 1971 Nike president Phil Knight paid Caroline Davidson, a local designer in the brand's home town of Portland, Oregon, $35 to design its 'swoosh' logo. It has gone on to become one of the most successful graphic identities ever produced. Whether on Michael Jordan's shoes, Pete Sampras's tennis shorts or Shane Warne's earring, wherever there is sport there is the Nike swoosh. Kids have had the logo cut into their hair, and even tattooed on to their bodies, so powerful has it become. In fact the swoosh became such a powerful symbol in its own right that Nike stopped printing its name underneath it and let graphic design speak for itself. The swoosh, however, may have become a victim of its own success. In a recent interview with Japanese design magazine *Idea*, John C. Jay, a creative director with Nike's main advertising agency Wieden & Kennedy, said 'Nike is concerned that the swoosh is being seen in too many places'. The company, he said, is to re-introduce the name Nike and drop its

Opposite: The Gray Nicolls cricket bat is clearly recognizable by its red stripe. Right: Despite the speed of Pete Sampras's service, there is no missing the Wilson 'W' stencilled on to his rackets.

distinctive trademark from some products.

The huge profits made by companies such as Nike, Adidas, Reebok and Umbro in the good years have, in turn, awoken sports teams to the vast profits that they can make from branded merchandise. The unique relationship between team and fan makes for the kind of brand loyalty marketers dream of. Football clubs now change their officially branded, sponsor-emblazoned kits every two years to satisfy demand from (or ruthlessly exploit, depending on how you look at it) their fans. It is worth noting that Barcelona stands virtually alone in not allowing its shirt to be sullied by a sponsor's logo. Elsewhere, dedicated club shops sell everything from underwear to bicycles emblazoned with the (official) club crest and colours. In the case of big clubs such as Manchester United, merchandising can account for more than half of annual income. Other sports have followed football's lead in getting their branding act together. Rugby Union, Rugby League and even cricket have spawned a plethora of graphic invention, all handily available in the club shop.

Of course, the real leaders in this sphere have always been American sports. Sales of team baseball caps, replica basketball jerseys and sweatshirts emblazoned with the name of a favourite American football team were booming long before football clubs had even thought about employing a marketing director, never mind a graphic designer.

American sports employ an entirely different graphic language to those of the rest of the world. Professional sport elsewhere revolves around clubs which have often developed out of local communities before becoming commercial professional organizations. Their identities reflect this, usually by incorporating coats of arms from town crests or symbols that have become associated with the team. Celtic and Rangers are both inextricably linked with communities with an enormously strong shared identity. Italy's AC Milan was started by Englishmen as a football and cricket club thus it is still called 'Milan' and not the Italian 'Milano'.

American professional sports teams, on the other hand, are commonly franchises given out by central administrative bodies such as the NBA (National Basketball Association) or NFL (National Football League). The three biggest team sports in the United States, American football, baseball and basketball, share a predilection for team names and iconography not found elsewhere in the world. Denver Broncos, Miami Dolphins, Detroit Pistons: American team identities are all about powerful, dynamic imagery mixed with local references.

Though the rest of the world may scoff at what could be thought of as ersatz gimmickry, the American concept is not a totally alien one. Most English football teams, for instance, have a nickname that uses very similar imagery to the names of American teams: West Ham are the Hammers, Norwich the Canaries, Leicester the Foxes, and team badges frequently pick up on these points of reference. But in America they have skipped the staid 'official' identity and gone straight for the emotional, fun, dynamic nickname. In the United States, Manchester United would be the Manchester Red Devils, Celtic, the Glasgow Shamrocks.

Previous pages:
Some of the highly
marketable and
easily identifiable
logos for the teams
in American Major
League Soccer
(MLS). Each team
identity was created
by marketing
professionals and
official kit suppliers
such as Adidas and
Nike. Opposite:
American golfer
Tiger Woods sporting
the Nike swoosh.

American sports teams thus find themselves with an easily identifiable, unique and highly marketable identity that has great appeal for kids. It is revealing to note that when the United States set up its latest attempt at forming a professional soccer league in 1996, Major League Soccer (MLS), the overwhelming majority of sides chose American-style team names such as New England Revolution or the Colorado Rapids rather than City, Albion or Rovers. The team identities are a peculiar clash of traditional football styles and American sporting iconography. There are the shields and balls familiar from clubs all around the world but also cartoon aliens, skyscrapers and even, in the case of The Columbus Crew, an illustration of three construction workers who look as though they are on their way to a Village People gig.

Each identity was created from scratch by the MLS working in conjunction with kit suppliers Adidas, Nike, Reebok and Puma. (This can be contrasted with the British experience where most club badges were created by a lecturer at the local art college or came about as the result of a competition in the local newspaper.) In the MLS launch media guide there is a short blurb explaining the thinking behind each design. Los Angeles Galaxy describe their identity thus:

'The logo system revolves around the one part of the cosmos that LA can rightfully claim: the sun. Spinning and energetic, the logo not only conveys the warmth and action of the city, but the intensity and movement of the game. The team's colours underscore the theme, while the retro typeface echoes art deco LA.'

In the United States team identities are all about powerful, dynamic imagery mixed with local references, for example, the Miami Marlins.

And for Dallas Burn: 'The logo system starts with the cowboy of the asphalt: the loners, outsiders and rebels found on cycle jackets and gas tanks. With a street-inspired aggressive typeface and a fire-breathing mustang, the Burn logo reflects the raw horsepower of the team and the speed of the gang – all mixed together in the combustion chamber of a hot Texas field.'

A hot Texas field may be a long way from a cold Lancashire mudpatch but this hyperbolic approach was recently adopted by none other than the grittiest of all sports, Rugby League. Australian media tycoon Rupert Murdoch has recently bought into the sport in a big way. His involvement caused a schism in the game in its biggest market, Australia, where clubs were split between joining his operation and staying with the existing Australian Rugby League. The Murdoch clubs formed their own competition, Super League, which was replicated in Britain.

In order to inject some new energy into the sport, and safeguard Murdoch's investment, the clubs involved were all relaunched with new kits and American-style identities. Bradford Northern became the Bradford Bulls while plain Wigan gloried in the fresh monicker of Wigan Warriors.

The relaunch has not met with universal approval. The importation of American marketing techniques has thrown up some glaring incongruities – the Leeds Rhinos? Not a beast commonly found roaming the streets around Headingley. The graphic language of American sports does not sit comfortably with the tough, working-class traditions of Rugby League. In importing and imposing such an alien culture, the game's

administrators are in danger of destroying part of what makes the sport special.

In Australia, the warring factions of Rugby League have now made up and launched a new competition, National Rugby League. When teams from the Murdoch operation play their old Australian Rugby League counterparts, the new and the traditional visual languages of the sport clash. The Murdoch teams adopted a corporate look to their shirts, designed by Nike. All the clubs wear a similar design, but in different colour combinations. Most of the old ARL teams, in contrast, still wear jerseys bearing familiar rugby graphic devices such as hoops and coloured 'V's. Their shirts have meaning that has built up over decades. Even their names – Balmain, South Sydney, Penrith – are redolent of a sporting culture that has great tradition. The Murdoch teams, with shirts that have

little that is distinctly rugby about their design and their Americanized names (Cronulla Sharks, Brisbane Broncos, Canterbury Bulldogs,) seem insubstantial and over-commercialized in comparison.

Similarly, market forces at work in football are endangering a visual language that is among the strongest of all sports. These stylings have emerged, for the most part, independently of the design industry and therefore have a special integrity, as a result of evolution rather than marketing. They are being undermined by the commercialization of the game. And the erosion of football's visual language threatens the culture of the game itself. Its distinctions from other sports become blurred. The targeting of middle-class fans and alienation of the sport's core as a result has led to worries over the erosion of the customer base that the game relies on in bad times. The destruction of the game's visual identity may result in damage to the culture which attracted the new money that has flooded into the game in the first place.

Recent signs are more encouraging with some manufacturers, notably Nike, returning to more traditional designs, but the lessons are there for other sports to beware of. Sport has, in the form of the graphics that surround it, some of the strongest visual languages in existence. They represent activities which are far more meaningful than mere leisure pursuits but which are distinct and unique. To a sport's follower such things as the design of their team's shirt embody tradition and history. We are in danger of homogenizing sports graphics to the extent that such meanings are lost. To tamper with them is to put the whole culture of sport at risk.

In early June 1998, just before the World Cup, three major British institutions were 'reshuffled': the Shadow Cabinet, The Spice Girls and the England Team. It was reverse order in the media coverage, however, because the England Team choice involved the Sacking of Gazza, Gazza's Drunken Binge, the Tears-of-a-Clown Gazza and the End of Gazza. Meaning that media at every class level gave it acres of space and miles of analysis. The previous week *The Times* had run a television-advertised, front-page exclusive interview feature: 'Danny Baker, The Gazza Interview'. Danny Baker and Gazza in *The Times*. That was how far it had gone... sports marketing.

Over the last ten years British sport has caught up with the notion of sports and sports stars as electronic intellectual property rights, walking sandwich-boards, celebrity endorsers, guarantors of media crossover, the province of the accountant and the marketeer. It is a big business. It's an American idea, of course, rooted in the conjunction of national network TV, pay-per-view big football and big sports agents like Mark McCormack, the man who made Arnold Palmer a multi-millionaire way back when. And the financial core of it, for the stars, the clubs and the agents was advertiser-supported media. That was how all the money

came in – the hundreds of millions of dollars from the official sponsors, and the incredibly expensive ad-breaks in the big games.

I watch at least three hours of television advertising at a stretch every week on a dedicated tape. I've written about advertising in the *Independent on Sunday* for the last four and a half years. Over that period – what we might call the 'Nick Hornby era' – I've seen the growth of sports marketing, through the Atlanta Olympics and the European Cup into the mad crescendo of the World Cup. As I write, at least one hour of this week's new advertising tape is taken up with sports-related advertising. It's the dominant single theme. As far as advertising is concerned, sport is the new rock and roll. Like rock and roll's transformation into the music industry, sport has been hugely professionalized, organized and mainstreamed to yield points of access and commercial exploitation just about everywhere, in every superstore, with every kind and condition of person.

Advertising uses sports themes and sports people to sell practically anything now – and some of the connections look extremely tenuous. So for instance Horlicks, the valetudinarian night-time drink, recently launched a new campaign with all the usual

womanly bedtime themes that ended dramatically with the footballer Les Ferdinand taking his clothes off. Horlicks is just one of a range of advertisers with absolutely no previously visible connection with sport, fitness, men or youth that has suddenly seen a new angle: spoof sex. Sports stars are extremely versatile – and there are so many of them to choose from, with such constant visibility. It makes sense, as they're mainly extremely famous, fit, good-looking ('uglies' get rooted out unless they are 'characters') young people with practically no cultural baggage whatsoever (except the loyalties attached to their teams and countries) who seem prepared to do absolutely anything. Much better than rock stars whose work, haircuts and tribal affiliations were universally divisive; who asked for ridiculous sums of money; and who made great fusses about the ethics of advertisers and wanted their own designers and make-up artists.

Young sports stars have risen without trace to form the infantry of B and C list celebrities, along with TV soap stars, weathergirls and second-rank musicians. If young women can see sports stars as sex objects, then grannies can think of conspicuously 'nice' stars, like footballer Gary Lineker, as grandsons; young

3 Selling an Attitude

Peter York

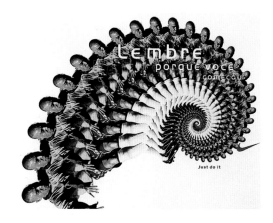

Lembre
porque você
começou

Just do it

Opposite: 'Do Running', outdoor poster campaign, 1997.
Advertising agency: Wieden & Kennedy, Amsterdam
Art director: John Norman and Harmine Louwe
Copywriter: Kathleen Lane
Client: Nike (European HQ, Amsterdam)

Left: 'Remember Why You Started', outdoor poster campaign starring Ronaldo 1997.
Advertising agency: Wieden & Kennedy, Amsterdam
Art director: Robert Nakata
Copywriter: Glenn Cole
Client: Nike (Brazil)

men can see them as idealized peer groups; early teens can see them as parents or older siblings and you can perm it any other way.

But the groups that most obviously idolize sports stars – and footballers in particular – are advertising creatives and their clients. Creative folk in British advertising pride themselves on their populist grasp of culture, their feeling for the great laddish themes of music, humour and sport. They are youthful themes with huge prestige in Soho where every creative imagines himself as a cross between Damien Hirst and James Brown (the former editor of *Loaded* magazine).

Sport has been made class-safe and aesthetically OK by the labours of a whole generation of middle-class pioneers from Brian Glanville – the thoughtful metropolitan bourgeois Jewish novelist-type who wrote broadsheet football criticism from the 1960s on – through to writer Nick Hornby. Hornby made it all possible for short, unathletic introverted middle-class 'boys' well into their thirties who wanted to identify with their football teams more than their wives, families or jobs. That top young sports folk now wear Gucci and Prada rather than Top Man certainly helped improve sport's image for a style-conscious audience.

Loaded magazine for superannuated lads, launched in 1993, really helped too. It recruited an astonishing number of readers no one in the magazine trade had realized were there to a diet of glossy populism that seemed football-driven, like its launch editor James Brown (*Loaded* presented the opposite side to the rather upmarket, solitary, meditative sports like climbing and Brazilian canoeing suggested by earlier men's magazines). *Loaded* covered popular sports, popular people, the lifestyle and drink. It had famous 'babes' taking their clothes off, rather than 'relationships'. It assimilated sport and sports people into its own version of Cool Britannia.

Loaded was a huge influence on the men's lifestyle magazine sector in general, which turned its focus rapidly to football, basketball and 'babes'. It also impinged on the wider media culture, and the self-image of young male journalists everywhere – and so, in very short order, on advertising creatives. Ad boys started to have football teams and little leagues. They wanted to know Ian Wright and Vinnie Jones as passionately as their predecessors had wanted to be part of the *Blitz* scene or make Brit films.

By happy coincidence for advertising men who like to feel that they are at the leading edge, sport, music and 'street-style' have grown increasingly close over the last ten years, united by the increasing dominance of black American dance music. This music, with its athleticism, its sport references, its dress code and, especially, its footwear codes, created an easy set of reference points which no advertiser or agency could ignore. If you wanted to add youth and vitality to almost any situation, sport and sports stars were the answer, and the rest of the package was easy to visualize (rap, kagouls, basketball caps – and the latest limited-edition training shoes).

The massive growth in the sports shoe market has driven everything in sports marketing over the last ten years. The real battle in the 1998 World Cup, according to the aficionados, wasn't the struggle between the national teams, but the fight between Nike and Adidas for the soul of the world's soccer-loving youth. A global, high-growth, high-margin fashion business like training shoes means huge advertising ratios and huge spends. Analysts reckon the main brands spent easily more than a billion dollars on advertising and sponsorship last year. And that is cultural influence at scale.

They've chosen to use it; sports shoe advertising has been some of the most

'Inner Strength', part of the print campaign to promote the TAG Heuer 'Kirium' watch. Herb Ritts was commissioned to photograph some of the world's top athletes, including the tennis champion Boris Becker and 100-metre hurdler Jacqui Agyepong.
Advertising agency: Bartle Bogle Hegarty
Photographer: Herb Ritts
Client: TAG Heuer

Below: 'Head to Head', print campaign featuring footballers Paul Ince and Les Ferdinand, 1997.
Advertising agency: Leagas Delaney
Creative Director: Tim Delaney
Photographer: Kurt Markus
Client: Adidas UK

Below: 'Dugarry', outdoor poster campaign for France Soccer, 1997.
Advertising agency: Wieden & Kennedy
Art director: Olivier Courtemanche
Copywriter: Ghislain de Villoutrys
Client: Nike, France

consistently visible work with the clearest creative and cultural agenda you could hope to find. The sports shoe brands are selling very powerful dreams – of escape, self-realization and peer group admiration – to children and young people. The agenda is to identify the major brands with relevant sports heroes, street style and music, in that order, and to make every pair – designed in the rich West, but mostly made in developing countries – into a message of hope.

If sports shoe advertising has forced the pace for sports marketing, then Nike has historically driven its sector. Nike is a story in itself (and they know it; it's the story they tell in their American theme-park shops, the Nike Towns). Nike comes from Portland, Oregon, the 1960s invention of a former university track sports star. And so too does its lead advertising agency, Wieden & Kennedy. One of the world's more influential marketeers has foregone Madison Avenue – even Chicago – for a small agency which has grown in a lop-sided way to Amsterdam and London, both European 'capitals of cool'. And the Nike output – initially all those basketball stars, tall, black and reaching for the skies – sent a new version of the classic American message. From Samuel Smiles through to Anybody Can Do Anything,

they would be saying 'Just do it'. Nike added the behavioural therapist's language and the unmistakable Nike tick (or 'swoosh').

Just do what? said the critics (and during the early 1990s period of gangsta rap and ghetto muggings and murders over new training shoes they said a whole lot more about that message). But the kids needed no translation and no excuses. With Nike you could walk as tall as you liked; with Nike the kid from the wrong side of the tracks could triumph and be cheered to the echo by friends in that freeze-frame moment of triumph. It was a message that echoed precisely what the big young-audience films of the 1980s – from *Top Gun* to *Flashdance* – had been saying.

If the sports shoe advertisers had clear objectives, a target market and a familiar set of messages in line with 'big picture' messages of the 1980s – and 1980s America in particular – none the less they developed a distinctive way of expressing them. Their agencies created advertising that looked and sounded different, and was very strongly branded in every frame, in every poster, in every magazine treatment. They created the very essence of sports hip, together with a celebration of the body.

Nike advertising is confident and distinctive because it appears to have been

conceived by people who had been inside their target market's central nervous system – knew how they thought and felt – and could relate to it. So Nike advertising dispenses with laborious explanation, obvious devices and plonky testimonials to concentrate instead on catching the feelings and the moments that matter. Nike advertising is transparent to the people it is aimed at – and often utterly opaque to people outside the target market.

When Tiger Woods appeared, seemingly breaking the mould of middle-aged, white American golf stars, Nike's commercial featured a variety of sub-teen boys, most of them black, saying 'I'm Tiger Woods'. Identification was the only thing that mattered. With basketball, an immensely important game in the United States with very wide participation – for the rest of the world, including the UK, it's still more symbolic than experienced – there is clearly a different approach, one that involves the viewer almost directly in the activity on the court. The camera angles, lighting and soundtrack are all directed to create the you-are-there atmospherics, and to involve the viewer with, say, Michael Jordan – one of Nike's key stars in a crucial period of its development – as a surrogate tribal big brother.

'Religion', cinema ad campaign for the British satellite broadcaster featuring Sean Bean, 1997.
Advertising agency: RSA
Art director: Barry Skolnick and John Gwyther
Copywriter: Barry Skolnick
Client: Sky Sports

With European soccer, Nike has followed a different tack, recognizing the extraordinary range of tribal emotions surrounding teams, locations and countries – and equally the dangers of trying to represent them literally. So the 'good versus evil' series, which was launched in 1996 at the time of the European Cup, used symbolism and fantasy to capture the collective emotions of team spirit and patriotism. It portrayed them using the oldest of narratives – the good guys against the devil/monster – and the newest techniques from the schlock-horror movies its audience watches. A team of international greats play the devil and his crew. Maldini passes to a flamboyant Brazilian and he passes to the increasingly famous 'interesting' Eric Cantona. Cantona does some dramatic business with his coat collar and a studied '*au revoir*' before shooting at a demonic goalkeeper whose leathery wings cover the goal. The ball then becomes a flaming planet, which proceeds to blow the creature up in approved horror-film fashion. Nike, in other words, had understood a different set of concerns and responded to them without losing their signature style.

Nike utterly dominated its sector until the early 1990s. It took the advertising initiatives with astonishing ease because it is, in

marketeers' jargon, an extremely focused brand with a very strong and consistent vision and personality. Nike is one of a small number of major new companies whose main assets are their brands and the relationships they command through marketing, rather than technologies or conventional skills.

But in the early 1990s Robert Louis-Dreyfuss, the entrepreneurial former chairman of Saatchi and Saatchi, moved to part-own and run Adidas, the world soccer-boot market leader, and utterly transformed the brand and its fortunes. Along the way he built a strong relationship with a much admired 'creative' London advertising agency, Leagas Delaney, who in turn developed an Adidas style, different from the Nike personality, but equally distinctive. Adidas' approach, while equally optimistic, substituted ideas and eclecticism for simple affirmation, aiming to be that bit cleverer and more authentic. The old simple Adidas shoes were revived as the 'real thing' for connoisseurs tired of Nike's neon overkill in its product design. And Adidas positioned itself closer to the product and its attributes and rather less as a brand celebrating itself.

Adidas TV commercials also tended to express, in one way or another, an alternative

to the big American takeover of youth culture. So we saw the boxer Prince Naseem go to conquer America with an almost religious mission; a Briton from Middle Eastern stock, Naseem is endorsed by a dreadlocked Jamaican in this commercial – a very 'Cool Britannia' theme – who says optimistically that all will fall before our Prince. The implication for some British viewers will have been that America is Babylon.

Another characteristic Adidas TV treatment takes the key modern opposition between the rhetorical claims of the new technology – Cyberhype – and the celebration of the body and outdoors; Adidas's world of The Natural High. In this elaborate fantasy a young prisoner in a kind of *Blade Runner* dystopia is forced to 'download himself' – to interface with electronic systems and become part of them. The story allowed Adidas to display a range of sophisticated references; an Uma Thurman lookalike interrogator and an inner life expressed by exterior symbolism somewhere between Michaelangelo and MTV. The whole ends in a classic alternative message: 'escape while you can'. With its own combination of topicality, fantasy and strong product stories, Adidas has built the other sports brand.

'Hang Time',
international TV ad
campaign starring
Spike Lee and
Michael Jordan,
1995. Nike signed
Jordan early in his
basketball career
to promote the Air
Jordan: it was the
most successful
trainer launch in
history.
Advertising agency:
Wieden & Kennedy
Director: Spike Lee
Client: Nike

But the story is much bigger than sports shoe brands – huge and influential as they are, sports themes get everywhere. Possibly the least interesting area of sports advertising is the real thing; advertising for real dedicated sports equipment and for real live sports events spectators. Many sports equipment markets are growing fast and big events are getting bigger but the advertising for them is out-spent and out-shone by the unreal thing – advertising for the most undedicated goods and services you can think of and advertising for media coverage of events.

The staple real equipment advertising on, say, Eurosport tends to be pretty pedestrian and traditional. Tennis stars have advertised rackets, strings and balls for ever and Pete Sampras – handsome but wooden – citing the virtues of Babilot strings by saying 'It's the best string that's made; that's why I use it', hardly belongs in the same universe as Nike and Adidas. Umbro, market leader in football strips, has a somewhat ambiguous position in all this. Football strips, as David Mellor can testify, are worn for real and unreal reasons by a great variety of people, some of them very young. The mix of motives between utility, display and tribalism is rich and thick. And Umbro can be a brilliant advertiser. They

produced a beautiful TV commercial around the time of the European Cup working the theme of heart and soul with an ad set in a well-observed but picturesque South American slum where everything hangs on the Big Match on TV. The moral – one I'll return to – is it's right for real people – that is, poor outsiders – to give their hearts to football.

But there's more to be seen outside the arena than in it. Because outside the arena some of the biggest advertisers in the world, bar none, have been muscling in on sports quite massively. Strongly child and teen-orientated advertisers like Coca-Cola, McDonalds and Pizza Hut – laddish but, objectively, profoundly unsporty – have bought up every relevant sportsman with a pulse. Pizza Hut has matey encounters in the Hut between clutches of footballers, and uses Damon Hill's woodenness and Murray Walker's madness to good effect. They subsume sports stars' sportiness in a more attention-getting laddishness – if they're your imaginary peer group, you're at the Hut table with them. It peoples the box – the standard Pizza Hut unit – with believable ghosts.

McDonalds interweaves the very famous in the lives of the very young. Thus McDonalds' sports treatment had Alan Shearer in

McDonalds buying Big Macs for his kids, paying with a cheque, and being asked by the blushing lad on the counter – who looked about fourteen – to provide a specimen signature. It's a standard advertising theme – magic people descending into unmagic places – usually played by celebrity actors. But the England captain means more to the teenage boy subset of McDonalds' market than any actor. Shearer's dad-like ordinariness helps make the whole thing consistent with McDonalds' new UK advertising theme of modern families.

Walker's Crisps made an inspired move in 1996 by hiring Gary Lineker, Britain's best loved profoundly nice person, to start a sustained series that identified him consistently with the brand and a memorable play on his niceness. The pleasant, greying Lineker is another ideal Dad-type, and the joke confirms his niceness by playing on it.

Another global advertiser that has taken up the sports theme in Europe is Coca-Cola. No longer working with one global American agency and campaign as it did in the 1970s and 1980s, Coca-Cola has incorporated football into its new language of authenticity. It shows real fans and matches in stylized ways and weaves them into a semi-religious incantation about

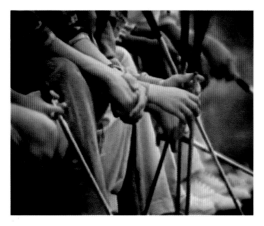

'I'm Tiger Woods',
international TV and
cinema campaign,
1997.
Advertising agency:
Wieden & Kennedy
Director:
Joe Pitka
Client: Nike

eating and sleeping football and drinking Coca-Cola, to a strong techno soundtrack, with ethnic-looking graphics. Like Umbro, Coca-Cola is making itself part of the fabric of fan-dom.

The media increasingly see sport as key to the building of 'brand personality'. The most dramatic, religiose appropriation of this kind came in a Sky Sports commercial (the first in a series of increasingly ambitious and expensive promotions), in which Sean Bean, actor and footballer *manqué*, strode about a football pitch describing the beautiful game as 'art, drama, religion, everything' to the fans, saying that we – meaning Sky – understood because we felt that way too. It was breathtaking in its cheek, its excess – Bean came across like the leader of the Peasant's Revolt or the Hitler Youth. The 'we understand' was presumably to underline Sky Sport's dedicated role for sports nuts – the kind of viewer who doesn't want their media diet interrupted by news, drama or documentary – as quite distinct from those unfocused, old terrestrial channels with their lucky dip offerings.

One terrestrial UK TV channel, Channel 4, however, is increasingly identifying itself with sports, particularly new, overseas and niche sports – from NBA basketball to Italian football – which it can make its own. Channel 4 has been promoting this part of its offering with a series of sponsored trailers branded by its sports sponsor, Volkswagen. These are shot and cut to look like arty European film shorts. The choice of sports and the style of promotion all reinforce Channel 4's identity as singular, leading-edge and youthful.

Newspapers, understandably, are less fussy and more short-term. Rather than using sports celebrities long-term to build brands and reader loyalty, their dedication to sports tends to have a week's shelf-life. They advertise to promote that week's big topical supplement, such as Wimbledon or the World Cup, using whoever is relevant and available. But there are more of these supplements around, and they're bigger, with more advertisers. They're seen as crucial to the future of newspapers and they command more of the newspapers' advertising budget. Increasingly they present newspapers as being about sports; part of the inexorable infotainment process moving newspapers towards 'soft' features and leisure.

But there's more on my tape; if sports and sports stars feature heavily and add their values to the advertising of trainers, media sports coverage and teen-targeted food and drink, that isn't the half of it. Sport themes and personalities turn up in an impossibly wide range of advertising. Kenny Dalgleish is just one of a range of celebrities endorsing the Bristol and West Building Society's dedication to mortgages, savings and investments. The strategy here is elusive. The Standard Life Bank uses a basketball player to illustrate its high rates of interest. The imagery of sports and fitness is so pervasive that it begins to symbolize a vast swathe of human endeavour – and add value and heroism to it.

As Robert Campbell, a leading London creative director, said: 'It's easy to sell a football script to a client. Everyone thinks football sells; it's the new safe thing to do.' Sports advertising involves clients in just this kind of safe, high-profile high-spend heroics. It's a role that can be parlayed into a lot of foreign trips, big parties and celebrity-hopping. With many sports sponsorships and themes, the heart rules the head and the sacred task of brand-building consistency gets lost in a boyish blur.

In the real world there has to be a backlash. *The Times* political feature writer Matthew Parris recently complained that sport exerted an unhealthy dominance in conversation. Why, he said, he'd even noticed that gay men had started talking about football as to the manner born. And he'd become a homosexual to get away from that kind of thing.

Below: Boddingtons 'Athlete', TV ad campaign, 1997, with Ken George and Melanie Sykes. Advertising agency: Bartle Bogle Hegarty Creative director: Bruce Crouch/ Graham Watson Art director: Simon Robinson Film director: Danny Kleinman Copywriter: Jo Moore Client: Whitbread Beer Company

'The Brief', TV ad campaign, 1997, with Ron Donachie and Lee Oakes. Advertising agency: J. Walter Thompson Client: Nestlé Rowntree

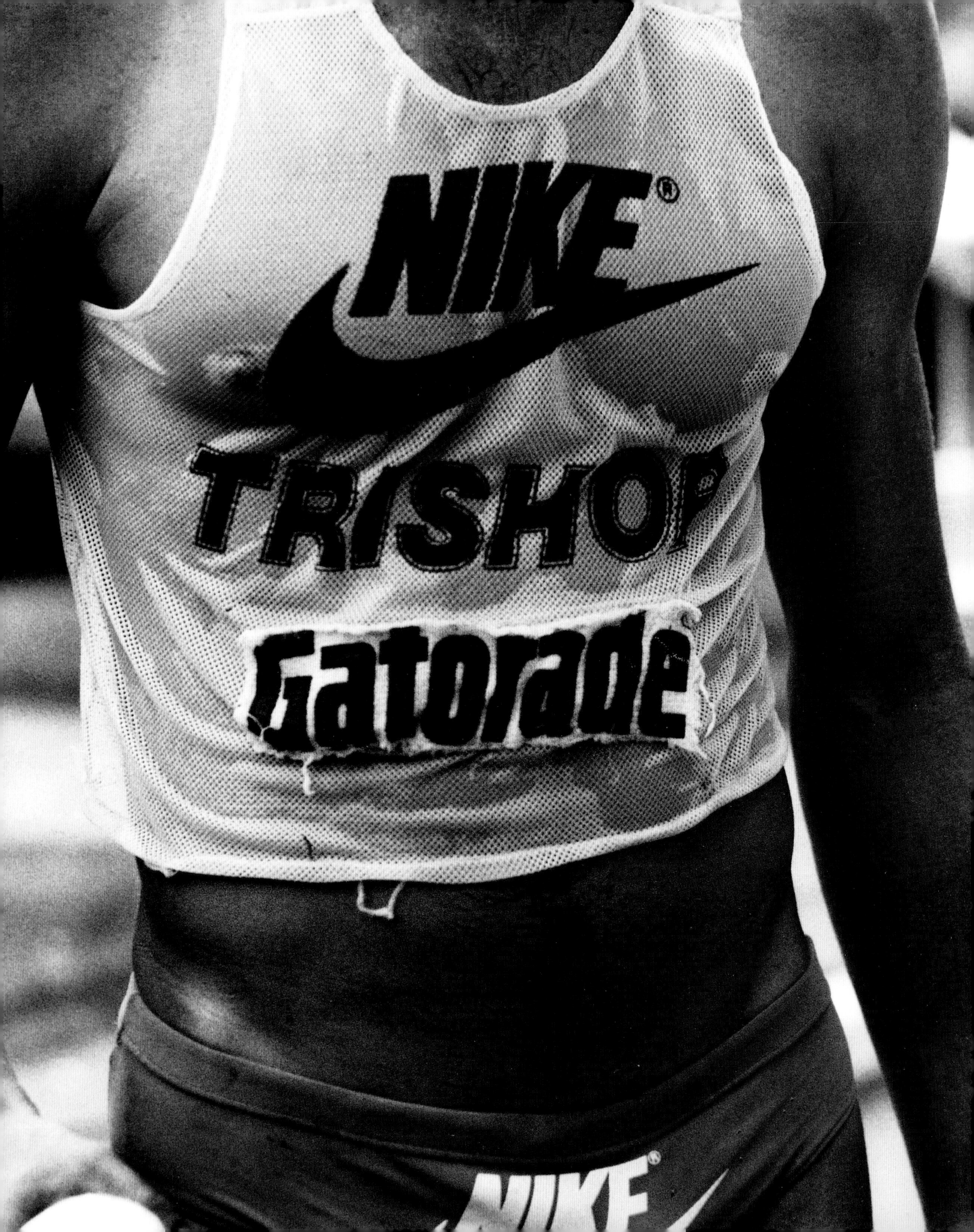
NIKE®
TRISHOP
Gatorade
NIKE®

'If Botticelli were alive today he'd be working for Nike.'
(after Peter Ustinov)

Los Angeles: the Sunday afternoon sun is dipping behind the extravagantly crenellated adobes of Beverly Hills. Along Rodeo Drive, long shadows fall across the candy-striped awnings of the designer boutiques as hordes of itinerant shoppers slope from window to window. Do we need that? Could we use that? Look, this one's even more expensive than the one next door. Having negotiated the doorways, they graze through the stores, their outsize cardboard carrier bags banging against their legs as they go.

Like most other cities in America, LA is now firmly attuned to Sunday shopping, though unlike New York, say, or Seattle or Chicago, shopping in Los Angeles is considered something of an art, particularly as it usually revolves around the consumption of the conspicuous and the superfluous. In LA, shopping in the 1990s is devotional, and although they give the impression of being collectively absent-minded, the hundreds of baseball-capped, Gap-legged and Nike-topped hill-billies strolling along Rodeo Drive and Wilshire Boulevard this winter afternoon have a collective purposeful glint in their eyes.

Nowhere is this glint more discernible than in Nike Town on Wilshire, along from the sumptuous Regent Beverly Wilshire hotel and close to Barneys and Saks. Here, these rich, doe-eyed Californians look as though they have died and gone to heaven. As sport has become the new religion, so Nike Town is its shrine. While Chicago and New York both have larger, more immediately impressive versions of Nike Town, the Los Angeles branch is no less intimidating. Here is a world that offers so much hope, in the shape of so much colour, so much speed, so many permutations of neoprene and at least 1,200 types of shoe. In the land of the single tick, all is sport, everything is image. There are six Nike Towns in the United States, and though the Chicago and New York stores are more like theme parks – bedecked with sports memorabilia, video walls and pre-recorded crowd noises – each outlet has the same expertly manufactured feeling of austere indulgence. In a comprehensive, rather remarkable way Nike has imbued consumerism with dignity.

This is why Nike Town is so popular with the sun-tanned deities of Beverly Hills. Here, training shoes and sweat pants are presented as choice exhibits in a travelling exhibition; jogging shorts and golf gloves have a reverential air about them; tennis socks and 'leisure' fleeces are displayed as though they are valuable works of art (which to Nike they kind of are). And not only do Nike instil their products with a certain holy superiority, they obviously infer that entry to this virtuous and meritorious world can be sanctioned simply by investing in a pair of Air Terra Woodlands or the Air Diamond Thief. When you put your foot into Nike's 'Ngage' laser machine and it not only gives you a readout of your foot's dimensions to the nearest millimetre, but also suggests compatible (Nike) products, then you know that you are one of the chosen, one of the great and the good, a member of Nike's seemingly inexhaustible army of consumer volunteers.

Opposite: Nike sponsors a number of individual athletes and teams, from Tiger Woods and Carl Lewis to the Brazilian football team – after all, young consumers like to wear what their sporting heroes wear.
Following pages: Nike made its money in basketball and the US jogging boom, but now that the market is saturated, it has targeted football as one of its core sports.

4
The Golden Fleece
DylanJones

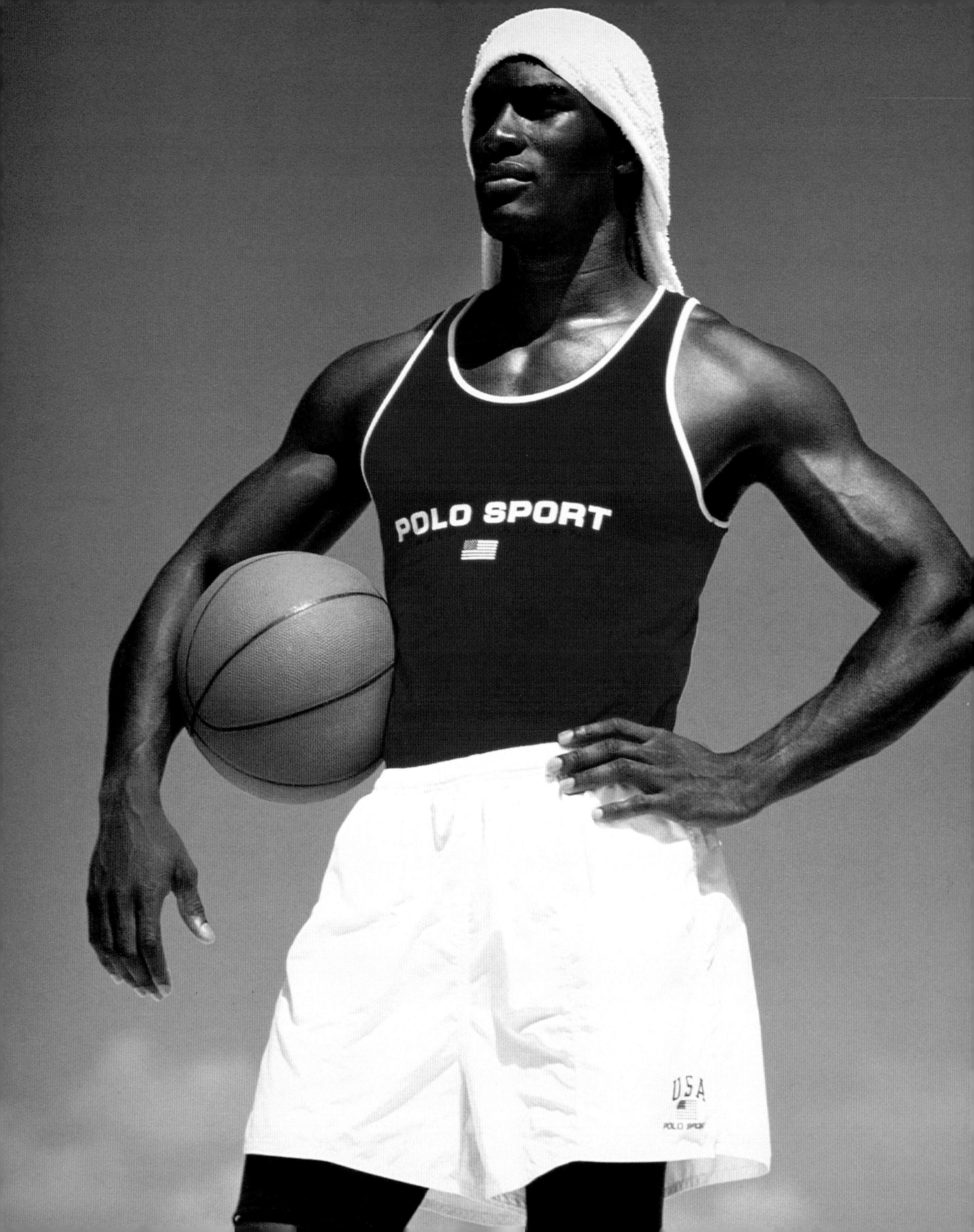
POLO SPORT
USA
POLO SPORT

Much has been made of the pervasive and occasionally pernicious influence of fashion in sport, and of sports in fashion, and considering that fashion is a culture – and now a medium – which venerates popular success, it is hardly surprising that the two have become so entwined. Sportswear, whether designer, athletic, or non-participatory, has been the predominant force in fashion design for the last ten years, as the industry, led by the United States, has striven to come to terms with a generational shift towards the casual and the ostensibly functional. You only have to walk into your nearest Calvin Klein/Ralph Lauren/Tommy Hilfiger/Donna Karan store to see that.

This boom happened not only because traditional sportswear companies tried to muscle into the world of designer fashion, but because those very same designers found it necessary to move into the world of sportswear. While designers frequently ape aspects of 'jock' culture, in the past these have tended to aspire to traditionally English, upmarket sporting pursuits. A late 1970s or early 1980s collection by, say, Giorgio Armani or Ralph Lauren will have included monogrammed blazers, cricket whites, hooped sailing tops, collegiate chinos, running shorts and perhaps a pair of hurriedly-rugged rubber-soled deck shoes. This was the East Coast writ large, Hampton playboys and Hollywood showgirls living it up under windswept skies in cotton and canvas. The name-brand designers only hit on real across-the-board success when they moved away from the 'prep' look and began developing downmarket,

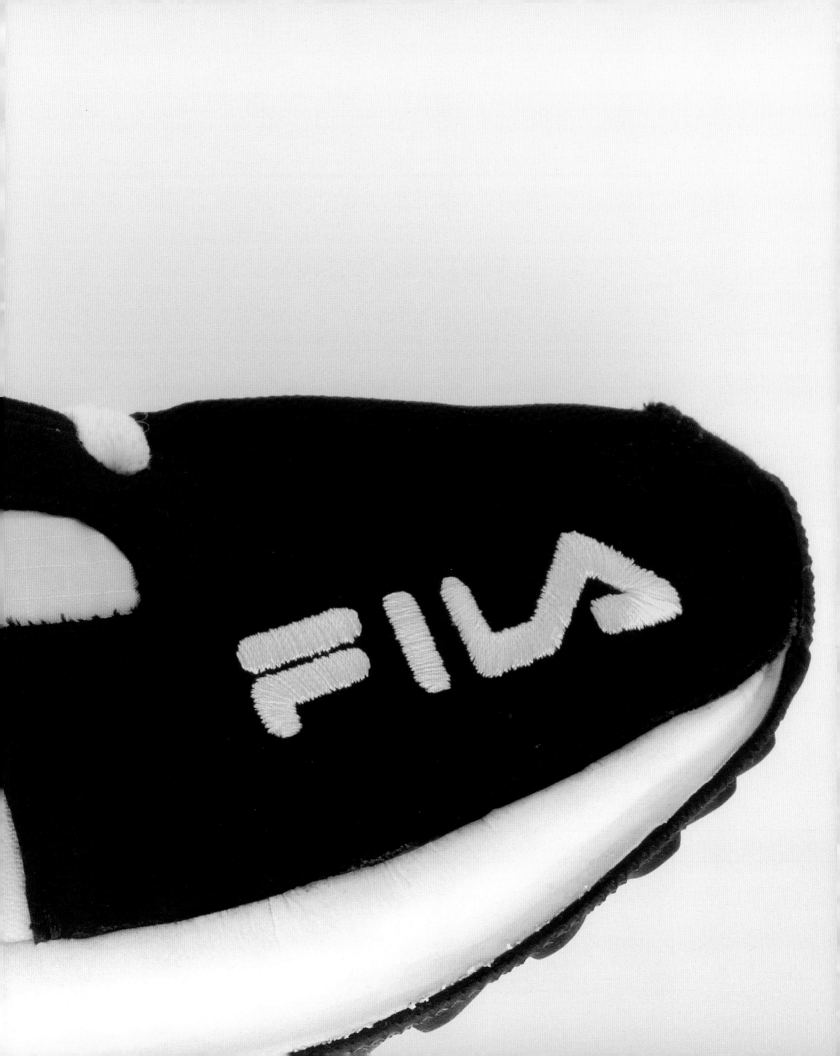

egalitarian sportswear which appealed to the hordes of dissolute yet fashion-obsessed youth who swore by their choice of trainers. In the 1980s, as rappers and professional athletes became the preferred role models for inner-city male youths, sport took on an increasing importance in culture, and sports-influenced style shifted from *haut monde* to *hoi polloi*.

The Autumn/Winter collections for 1998 showed how this phenomenon has increased: hooded gabardine sweatshirts from Prada's new technical skiwear line, sporty Velcro fastenings from Jil Sander, leather football boots from Louis Vuitton and skateboarding-inspired cashmere zip-fronted cardigans from Marc Jacobs; the only jewellery required being a cute Casio sports watch. Even couture houses have appropriated the technologically advanced fabrics of track and field: Polartec fleece, neoprene, Gore-Tex and cyber-Lycra.

Successfully fusing the street with the chic has pushed the American fashion designer Tommy Hilfiger's personal fortune to over $150 million. Up until the early 1990s, the three-ring circus of American fashion was dominated by the designer demi-gods of Fifth Avenue: Calvin Klein, Ralph Lauren and Donna Karan. And while they still dominate, they have recently been joined – upstaged, some would say – by Hilfiger. Since hooking up with the Hong Kong investor Mohan Murjani in 1984, the New York-born designer has turned his company into a marketing powerhouse, targeting the youth market with alarming accuracy. His trick was the juxtaposition of two major American styles –

mixing blue-blooded conservatism with hyper-kinetic urban casual wear; Hilfiger is where jock meets nerd meets rapper meets ski-bum. He called it 'prep-tech', and his collections include brightly coloured, brazenly logoed sailing jackets, puffy jackets and ski-pants as well as Ivy League staples such as chinos and button-down shirts.

For young black America for the last three years the Hilfiger logo has become a sartorial icon, perhaps the hippest label in the whole of the United States. So hip, in fact, that the designer has been name-checked in hip-hop tenement operas by the likes of Mobb Deep, Grand Puba and Chef Raekwon. This appreciation has spread to Europe and in particular to Britain, where readers of youth style magazines such as *i-D* and *The Face* see Hilfiger as the acceptable face of corporate streetwear. Last year Hilfiger made over $1.3 billion, wholesale.

The status of pop singers or movie stars as the most convincing secular heroes is being challenged by sports people. Predictably, it was Nike who played an intrinsic part in their elevation to demi-god status; Nike who made sports fashionable. In November 1978 the *Washington Post* ran a story claiming that Nike was paying college basketball coaches to use their shoes, or at least were supplying them with free shoes to be given to their players. While Nike had not actually broken any rules, the publicity was enough to scare their competitors – namely Adidas, Converse, Pro-Keds and Puma – into downplaying any player endorsements and recruitments they might have had. Nike, meanwhile,

Below: Mel C of British pop band The Spice Girls, known as Sporty Spice, influenced teenage girls with her penchant for Adidas tracksuits. Opposite: The Adidas Warp shoe has zig-zag lace styling and a contoured, rock-climbing shape.

had to consider their options; they could retreat and keep quiet, or they could move on regardless. They had already been painted as mercenaries in the case, and it was possible that the worst of the bad publicity was over. Consequently, Nike made an all-out push to sign more coaches and players while the competition was lying low, snapping up everyone in sight, providing much of the groundwork that eventually led to relationships with global, monolithic stars such as Michael Jordan, Bo Jackson and Mary Decker Slaney.

In the modern digitally arranged world it is far, far cooler to want to be Michael Jordan or Shaquille O'Neal than it is Liam Gallagher or Richard Ashcroft. Basketball players, football players, sprinters and baseball stars have another sphere of influence, as well as being categorically entwined with youth, whereas pop and movie stars often only offer the semblance of youth. Endorsing sport and sportswear has adolescent associations: by swathing yourself in the designer labels of the potentially active – Nike, Reebok, Adidas, Converse, Fire & Ice, Spalding, Stylo, North Face, Northwave – you are immediately placed in the 18–34 demographic, even if to the outside world you are an overburdened, overweight fortysomething.

And because sports are now deemed to be tremendously fashionable, they have cycles of popularity, much like music used to. In Britain in the late 1970s there emerged a kind of musical cherry-picking; every six months there would be a media-driven re-evaluation of the music scene. Twenty years later, we apply the same principles to sport, with golf being the most recent, and most unlikely candidate. What

began a few years ago as a slacker pastime enjoyed in an ironic low-boredom-threshold-type way by white hip-hop boys, became a genuine fashion movement – quickly exploited by the likes of Paul Smith, Polo Ralph Lauren, Salvatore Ferragamo, Emporio Armani, Kangol and Antonio Miro. When Tiger Woods suddenly became a media icon, golf was elevated to a bonafide cultural phenomenon.

The fetishism associated with designer sportswear certainly didn't begin with golf, but rather with Fred Perry and René Lacoste, who started putting their logos on the breasts of their open weave piqué tennis shirts, Perry using a laurel-wreath insignia and Lacoste a crocodile, after his nickname. The Lacoste Company in particular was responsible for a minor revolution in men's sportswear.

Opposite: The Fred Perry logo. Below: René Lacoste invented the Lacoste polo shirt in 1933. It was made of a new fabric – called piqué – that was able to keep sweat away from the body far better than the wool jersey or woven cotton which prevailed in tennis whites.

Above: Fred Perry winning the Wimbledon Men's Singles Championship in 1935 wearing his laurel-wreath insignia tennis shirt. Following pages: Fashion shoot featuring sportswear by Dolce & Gabbana, Giorgio Armani, Lacoste, Nicole Fahri, No Fear, O'Neill, Paul Smith, Polo Ralph Lauren, Quick Silver, and Trussardi Jeans (page 96). Fleece, the 100 per cent polyester fabric once worn only by explorers, mountaineers and ramblers, is now a popular feature of catwalk and high-street fashions (page 97).

Launched in 1933, its dedication to logo branding meant putting its crocodile motif on key-rings, hats and shoes. Lacoste eau de toilette appeared in 1968, Lacoste sunglasses were first marketed in 1979, sportsbags in 1981, the Lacoste Peugeot 205 was launched in 1984 and the ultimate lifestyle toy, the Lacoste 42 sailboat, was built in 1985. Nike has obviously taken this concept to a new, previously unimaginable pan-global level in terms of market saturation and media complicity, yet it was the French tennis champion and two times Wimbledon winner who had helped them find the ladder.

The Nike 'swoosh' and the three stripes of Adidas have now joined red Coca-Cola cans and the McDonalds yellow 'M' in a holy quartet of recognizable global symbols, part of the everyday landscape of popular consumerism. Nike – the Greek goddess of victory – is still the brand leader, boasting a 33 per cent share of the world's trainer market (40 per cent in the United States), yet Adidas is quickly gathering speed, particularly in the area of 'peer cool', which is a very important area indeed. The Spice Girls' Mel C – indubitably the sassiest, coolest Spice – indoctrinated an entire generation of teenage girls with her penchant for Adidas tracksuit bottoms, the ones with the three-stripe logo and the double ring halfway round the calf.

Fashion, in much the same way as any other part of popular culture, is blessed with built-in obsolescence, and the design and marketing of training shoes has turned obsolescence into something of an art. They're like buses: you don't see one for 40 years and then several hundred all come along at once. Now they come in all shapes, for every occasion: bigger, blacker, sleeker, slighter; big clumpy shoes for snowboarders; slim 'street shoes' for golfers; multi-purpose pumps for use on trains and boats and planes. Training shoes aren't ubiquitous, they're *air*, all around us, all of the time. 'If the automobile captured the popular imagination of the Fifties, symbolizing the new prosperity of that time,' says Steven Langehough, from the Cooper-Hewitt Design Museum in New York, 'today the athletic shoe has become a more democratic symbol of identity and prestige in multi-cultural America.'

Journalists talk about a new training shoe the way they used to talk about genre-busting pop music or difficult art, using postmodern analogies (now invariably invoking aerodynamics), high fashion lingo, anything to elevate these fastidiously designed pieces of rubber to...what, exactly? *American Vogue's* Robert Sullivan found this to say about Nike's new Air Terra Humara: 'A shoe with the sort of nautilus-like shape of a camera's shutter; a shoe like the kind of long lever that clicks along the teeth on the gear of a clock; the hub of a very cool wheel... The longitudinal slits sing of side-to-side stability.' Even their names are subject to intense scrutiny. 'The genus and species names were easy,' writes Sullivan: 'Air for Nike, and Terra for ground. Humara, according to the marketing department, came from the Humara Indian tribe, based in Texas, which was known to partake in long off-road runs: "Finding relevant names is probably one of the most difficult challenges we have. We use a lot of Swahili."'

Previous pages: As the traditional sportswear companies have moved into designer fashion, designers have increasingly introduced sportswear into their collections. Page 98: Yohji Yamamoto, Spring/ Summer 1997. Page 99: Red or Dead Autumn/ Winter 1998. Pages 100–102: Tommy Hilfiger Spring/Summer 1997. Page 103: Yohji Yamamoto Spring/ Summer 1992.

Below: Trainer by DKNY. Opposite: Close-up of Helmut Lang fabric.

HELMUT LANG JEANS

M. _____

PRODUCED IN 1996

But maybe, just maybe, the market has reached saturation point, as Nike – still the market leader with sales in 1997 of over $9 billion – recently, astonishingly, posted two profit warnings. Of course, this could be a mere blip, although the trend is away from trainers towards 'brown shoe goods', the hybrid training/ walking outdoor boots manufactured by companies like Caterpillar, Timberland and Rockport (who are owned by Reebok). In 1997, Rockport's turnover was $500 million.

Again, this is a trend determined by street style, like so many before it. In the early 1980s, 'casuals', young, male, working-class football supporters, displayed parochial and fiercely partisan relationships with sporting manufacturers such as Tacchini, Fila and Adidas which made them seem as though they belonged to some kind of secret order (Liverpool football fans even travelled to Europe to buy particular Adidas trainers unavailable in Britain). Here was a small, enormously influential world populated by marginalized white youth, a world where sporting the right Pringle jumper or the wrong pair of jeans could turn you into a terrace messiah or a social outcast in the space of an afternoon. These talismanic polo tops, sweaters, windcheaters and track pants were soon gobbled up by the fashion industry which went to great pains to build them into their own parallel world, wearing them to nightclubs, using them in fashion shoots and mixing them with haute couture in catwalk shows.

In the 1990s, this juxtaposition is *de rigueur* in music, advertising, fashion, everything. Acknowledging the defining principles of street-sportswear is a sure road to success. In 1992 the art director Peter Saville produced a catalogue for the formerly inscrutable Japanese fashion designer Yohji Yamamoto, using cutting-edge magazine people such as photographer Donald Christie and stylist Melanie Ward. 'The women's collection was brilliant: Yohji sent everything down the runway with Nike trainers and it reminded me of an American woman I'd seen in Europa Foods in Notting Hill one night, in a blue raincoat and trainers,' says Saville. 'It was that New York street look. We shot clothes on 35mm and video and we went to Europa, we went under the Westway, we went to Brixton and gave the clothes to skateboarders.' Yamamoto loved it: 'Peter, you gave a £2,000 silk dress to a girl for basketball. I like it.' No matter how incongruous this might seem – and it is totally incongruous – ironic juxtapositions are the mainstay of creative fashion imagery, but now we are seeing ballgowns and trainers instead of dinner suits and hobnails.

As Nike's sales figures show, however, irony is hardly the reason why logo-driven, adrenalin-boosting sportswear is the order of the day, whether by reputable sports manufacturers or high-end fashion designers (whether on a catwalk or a rock face). Performance sportswear – by which we mean the type of things manufactured for snowboarding, hiking, sailing, mountainbiking, rockclimbing and alpine sports – is everywhere these days, with labels such as Stone Island, CP Company, Massimo Osti's Left Hand, Helly-Hansen, Karrimor, Berghaus, Patagonia, Henri Lloyd and Musto producing outdoor

clothes like fleeces, waterproof jackets, rainproof blousons and ski-tops that have become mainstays of street clothing and magazine fashion.

As the sportswear market grows, so the spoilt consumer becomes more literate as well as more demanding. Even if we are not the least bit athletic, we demand the latest high-performance fabrics, products and designs. Companies such as Karrimor have exploited this. From its Lancashire roots as a maker of panniers for post-war cyclists, the company built up a reputation for beautifully produced if slightly dull outdoor clothing. Two years ago it was bought by Italian holding company 21 Invest, who embarked on a massive repositioning exercise. Now Karrimor is the leading producer of outdoor artefacts, its flagship products being ergonomically designed rucksacks in Kevlar and rip-stop nylon. It has even given rise to a fashion term: technocool.

Nautica is very technocool. An American yachting label that has merged function and fashion for the last 15 years, Nautica considers technical innovation something of a crusade. Last year it launched both Nautex – a water-repellent, windproof counterpart to outdoor stalwarts like Gore-Tex – and Nautech fleece, which is compact, soft and lightweight with all the properties of Polartec 100, the heat-retentive fleece fabric responsible for the 1990s alternative to the designer sweatshirt.

The 'performance' market is evolving quickly, and to stay smart you have to monitor the sector closely. Paul Smith knows this, and was mindful of the me-too syndrome when he recently introduced his Urban Trackers line (part of the PS Jeans range) which is notionally for mountaineering. 'There's been such a lot of so-called performance wear around recently with all those shiny fabrics and flashy colours at the designer end of the market,' he said at the launch. 'I wanted to produce something a little more realistic.' As the performance market becomes more sophisticated, so the goods follow suit; both Polo Sport and Nautica have dulled down their collections, worried that they might seem to be a little too logo-conscious. This has not yet filtered down to the high street, which is still awash with the logo-centric camouflage of sofa-sized, gun-toting gangsta rappers, down-filled people who look like hand grenades designed by Claes Oldenburg. Everywhere you look there's a pair of Air Jordans or Puma GV Specials.

Sportswear has infiltrated the office, the home, the street. Not only are logos everywhere, we have *become* logos, parading ourselves as if we were sponsored peacocks. In some ways we have stopped growing up and have reverted to childhood. Magazines have found a 'middle youth'; those who have prolonged adolescence into middle age. After all, shopping is something learnt when young but perfected with age. Especially these days.

Which is how we came to be walking down Wilshire Boulevard, towards Nike Town, intent on serious Sunday afternoon grazing. We're about to invest in seriously lurid, logo-intensive golfwear. It's neat. Never seen it before. Looks cool. Looks *really* cool. Could wear it at the beach next weekend. And it's all so new. Why not? We think we'll buy two of everything. Like we did last week.

Below right: The current trend in sports footwear is a move away from trainers towards 'brown shoe goods', a combination of outdoor footwear and sports footwear technology, produced by companies such as Caterpillar, Timberland and Rockport. Opposite: The Adidas Badlander (1998).

THE GREAT STADIUM
SHEPHERD'S · BUSH · LONDON

THE OLYMPIC GAMES 1908

PROGRAMME

The Olympics have been the forcing ground for architectural expressions of sport: partly functional machines designed for the speediest translation of crowds from gate to seat and back again, and part triumphal containers, intended to celebrate the supremacy of one city over another. But they have not been the only focus. In the United States, football and baseball have been the catalyst for a generation of stadia employing new technologies which have allowed for continual expansion in the size of sports auditoria, as well as the possibility of keeping the worst of the weather, hot or cold, at bay. In Europe, soccer has been no less important. When Italy staged the World Cup it set a standard with a raft of specially built – or expanded – stadia from Milan to Bari. And France was of course eager to trump Italy in 1998. The Stade de France was the result of a major architectural competition, one that was mystifyingly not won by Jean Nouvel, even though he did all he could to secure the commission

Opposite: Programme for the 1908 Olympic games, London.

5
The Arena
Martin Pawley

'When we speak of ancient Olympia we assume it is understood that it was composed of two distinct parts. The *Altis* or sacred precinct was Olympia properly speaking. Outside and all around it stretched the profane city, the abode of the hoteliers and tradesmen. Such an arrangement should be preserved to ensure that the athlete's accommodation, the restaurants, the annexes of all kinds are kept on the outskirts away from the court of honour and without a direct link to the heart and centre.'
Baron Pierre de Coubertin (1863–1937) Creator of the modern Olympic games

Once upon a time sport was illegal. In the seventeenth century *The Book of Sports*, a royal proclamation asserting that it was not a sin to sport after church on a Sunday, so upset the puritans that it became a contributory cause of the English Civil War. After the war the victorious Roundheads called in all copies and had them publicly burned. Sport was banned until the restoration of 1660. For the next 200 years it became a matter of amateur fun and games accompanied by gambling on the outcome. It was not until the twentieth century that sporting pastimes became truly professional and the science of winning was born.

Today sport is the approved lubricant of international relations and the accepted arena for communal rivalries. But as competition has improved performance, and performance has improved training, and training has bred

professionalism, the setting in which sports take place has become increasingly important. Professionalism, training, experience and performance all have analogues in architecture, where the same qualities are prized. In the most spectacular arena of the sports calendar, the Olympic games, the architecture of the setting reflects the Olympic motto – cirtus, altius, fortius (faster, higher, stronger). The architecture of the Olympic stadium has become part of the identity of the games: a star in its own right, an event in itself, an achievement at the centre of winning.

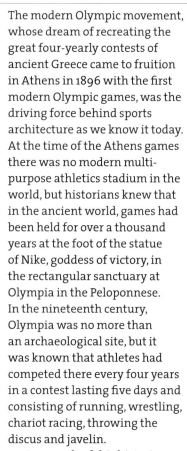

Athens
1896

London
1908

The modern Olympic movement, whose dream of recreating the great four-yearly contests of ancient Greece came to fruition in Athens in 1896 with the first modern Olympic games, was the driving force behind sports architecture as we know it today. At the time of the Athens games there was no modern multi-purpose athletics stadium in the world, but historians knew that in the ancient world, games had been held for over a thousand years at the foot of the statue of Nike, goddess of victory, in the rectangular sanctuary at Olympia in the Peloponnese. In the nineteenth century, Olympia was no more than an archaeological site, but it was known that athletes had competed there every four years in a contest lasting five days and consisting of running, wrestling, chariot racing, throwing the discus and javelin.

As a result of this historic connection the first modern games took place in the so-called 'Panathenian Stadium', the excavated 'U'-shaped marble stadium of Herodes Atticus dating from 331 B.C., restored and enlarged to accommodate 60,000 spectators by Greek architect Anastasios Metaxes.

The pioneers of the modern Olympic movement were driven by elevated ideals drawn from classical history. Baron Coubertin, founder of the International Olympic Committee and father of the Athens games, aimed for a cultural reunification of art and sport in a spiritual setting, uncontaminated by politics or commerce. He believed there should be few if any spectators, but few of the promoters who bid for Olympic committee endorsement shared this view. The games following 1896 took place in Paris in 1900 and Saint Louis, Missouri, in 1904, both of them coupled with international exhibitions. These games were considered less than satisfactory by the Olympic movement, not least because they incorporated events – such as 'anthropological contests' between different races held in Saint Louis – that would not be considered acceptable today. Coubertin wrote to his followers: 'The games must be more dignified; more discreet; more in accordance with classic and artistic requirements; more intimate and, above all, less expensive.' Most of his wishes, particularly the last, were destined not to be fulfilled.

The fourth modern Olympic games took place in London in 1908 in a specially designed venue: the White City exhibition ground and stadium on the western edge of the city. The site area exceeded 40 hectares (100 acres) and the stadium, designed by the architect James Fulton, consisted of a large grass infield circled by parallel-sided stands, half-circular at each end. The stands themselves were a single tier of seating framed in steel with two parallel covered sections, the whole capable of accommodating over 80,000 spectators. Though these

facilities were impressively large, the stadium had disadvantages from the point of view of athletic performance. Spectators seated in the stands were obliged to overlook a running track and a concrete cycle track with banked turns before they could see the infield events – which for the first and only time in the history of the Olympics included swimming and diving, events subsequently removed to a separate location. After the games, the White City stadium became a popular equestrian and dog racing arena until its demolition in the 1980s.

Stockholm
1912

Los Angeles
1932

The next Olympic games was held in Stockholm in 1912. Once again attention centred on a purpose-designed stadium, this time a 22,000-seat structure by the architect Torben Grut. This design was considered so successful that the International Olympic Committee decided that all proposals for future games would include a new stadium. By the end of 1913 an earth stadium designed by architect Otto March had already been constructed in the Berlin suburb of Grünewald for the games of 1916, cancelled because of World War One.

From the standpoint of planning and design, the two most important Olympic games of the first half of the twentieth century took place in the 1930s: the Los Angeles games of 1932 and the Berlin games of 1936. The Los Angeles games, held at the lowest point in the world economic depression, none the less led to the construction of the largest stadium in the world, the 100,000-seat Memorial Coliseum designed by the father and son team of John and Donald Parkinson. This epic brick and concrete structure – the last open-ended horseshoe design to be built for any Olympic games – occupied 12 hectares (30 acres) of the city's Exposition Park and was so successful that it was used again in the second Los Angeles Olympics of 1984. The Los Angeles games of 1932 also saw the first ever inclusion of a purpose-made Olympic village, which provided spartan accommodation for athletes from 37 nations, and the use of a large number of widely distributed sites. Because of the excellence of its planning as well as the international style of its architecture, the setting created for the Los Angeles games of 1932 appears modern even today.

Following pages: General view of the swimming pools in the stadium for the 1936 Olympic games, Berlin.

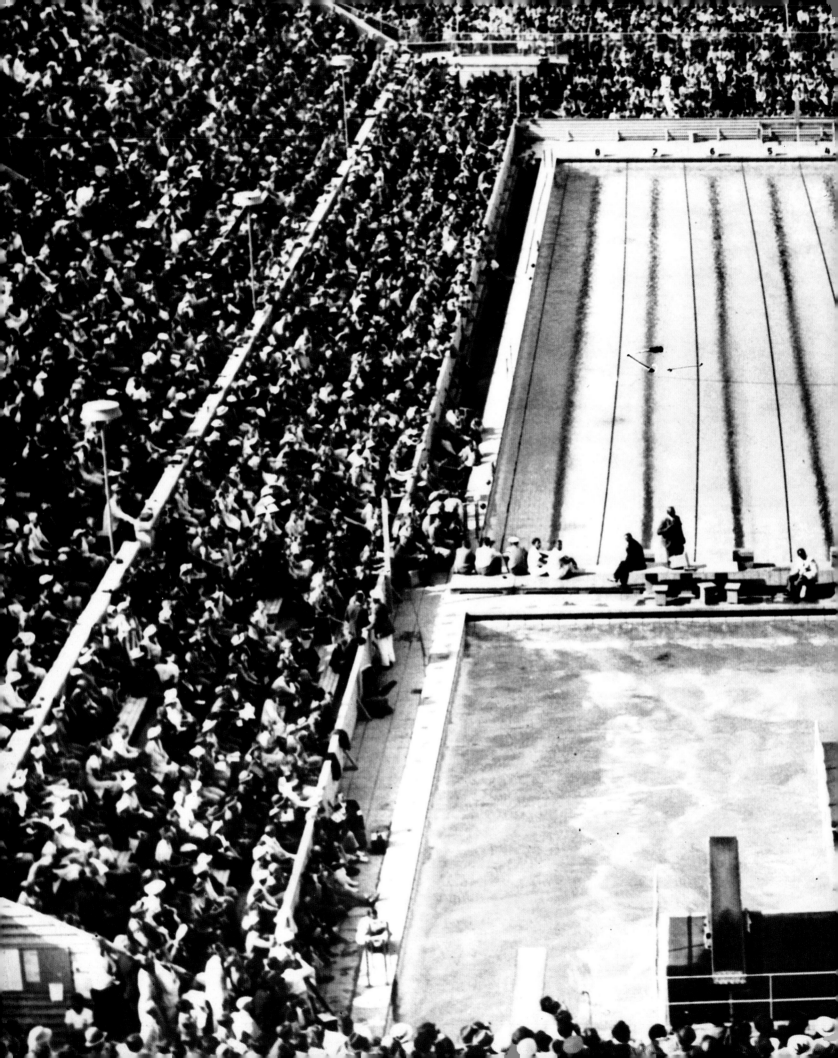

Berlin
1936

The Berlin Olympics of 1936 built upon the success of Los Angeles but in a very different way. Held three years into the Nazi era, the brief for the reuse of the Grünewald site called for the demolition of the unused 1913 earth stadium as part of a general clearance inspired by the success of the sprawling Los Angeles masterplan. But where the Los Angeles Olympic attractions had been spread over 259 square kilometres (100 square miles), the elements of the Berlin plan were concentrated into less than a quarter of that area, a planning decision that necessitated a close architectural relationship between all the main buildings and public and performance spaces. By far the largest element in the resultant composition was the Olympic stadium designed by the Berlin Olympic Committee's own architect, Werner March, son of the designer of the 1913 stadium. March's vast, stone-clad, colonnaded oval comfortably exceeded the capacity of the Los Angeles Coliseum by providing seating for 110,000 spectators but, because its turf infield was sunk some 12 metres (40 feet) below ground level, it appeared less dominant and by this means integrated itself into the total composition of the site in a very satisfactory way. Surrounding support areas and structures like the Maifeld, the Langemarck Hall and bell tower, the swimming arena and the promenade were all arranged on plan so as to provide classic vistas in all directions with a welcome absence of unplanned small-scale buildings. Taken as a whole, the Olympic setting was a processional achievement that culminated in the revelation of the interior of the stadium itself, which always appeared larger and deeper than arriving spectators expected.

Architectural composition was not the only success of the Berlin Olympics. In addition to the restraint, harmony of materials and integration of design elements, new dimensions were added to the Olympic experience that reached beyond the stadium in novel ways. Not only was the entire games filmed by the director Leni Riefenstahl – later to be released as a full length feature entitled *Olympische Spiele* – but throughout the summer of 1936 the German dirigibles Graf Zeppelin and Hindenburg, decked out with huge Olympic rings painted on their sides, carried the message of the games on scheduled passenger flights to North and South America, and also flew over the stadium while the games were in progress.

Were it not for its continued association in the public mind with the rise of Fascism – the war against which was to be the cause of the abandonment of the Olympiads of 1940 and 1944 – the architectural backdrop to the games of 1936 would almost certainly be regarded as the apogee of pre-television Olympic design. In Berlin all the positive elements of previous Olympic games were present and brought together, including a state-of-the-art stadium, a separate swimming arena and an Olympic village. At the same time (as in Los Angeles), the entire Olympic project served as a public works programme that helped reduce unemployment and encourage German manufactures. The charge of permitting political interference in the conduct of the games that is frequently levelled against the Berlin Olympic Committee may be justified, but interference of this kind did not end in 1936. It continued in the conduct of the post-World War Two superpowers in all matters relating to the Olympics up to the end of the Cold War in 1989.

Opposite: Entrance to the stadium for the Berlin Olympics.

Helsinki
1952

Rome
1960

After Berlin, the Olympic movement took time to adapt to a new era. In 1948 the games returned to war-torn London using the exhibition stadium at Wembley that had been built for the British Empire Exhibition of 1924. Four years later the Helsinki games, the first to be televised internationally, also made use of an existing stadium, a 25,000-seat reinforced concrete structure designed by architects Yrjo Lindegren and Toivo Jannti for the abandoned 1940 games. Preserved through the war and then enlarged, by 1952 it could accommodate 70,000 people.

Apart from the preservation and enlargement of its modern stadium, the Helsinki games' main contribution to Olympic design was in the dramatization of its architectural setting. At the opening ceremony, the bearer of the Olympic flame made a circuit of the stadium before handing the torch to the first of a series of runners who carried it up the open staircase of a 72-metre (236-foot) reinforced concrete observation tower to ignite the

Olympic cauldron at the top. Variations on this piece of 1952 theatre were to reverberate through the design of Olympic settings in the years ahead.

Since the beginning of the modern Olympic revival the number of athletes taking part had steadily increased. Only 311 took part in Athens, while 5,867 competed in Helsinki. But as the competition grew more intense, so did the politics. The Soviet Union, which had declined to take part in any Olympic games until Helsinki – where its athletes demanded their own separate Olympic village – thereafter became a gold medal contender and initiated a battle for supremacy with the United States that ended only with the collapse of the USSR. Another change came about as a result of the growing importance of television coverage and creation of a mass global audience for the games. This was to generate a massive income for holders of the games, as well as influencing forever the design function of Olympic architecture.

Opposite: The Palazzetto dello Sport, engineered by Pier Luigi Nervi for the Rome Olympics. This arena is generally regarded as the best building of the Rome games.

After Helsinki the Olympiad fell to Melbourne, but apart from an Olympic pool by architects Borland, McIntyre and Murphy – the first indoor swimming arena purpose-built for the games – the architecture of 1956 fell short of expectations. This was not the case in Rome in 1960. The Italian city responded to the challenge with unprecedented investment. There were new sports buildings, hotels, road links, a new airport and a new municipal water supply. Although the main Olympic buildings were modern, wrestling took place in the Basilica of Maxentius and gymnastics in the Baths of Caracalla. Economies too were effected in the Olympic village, a 1,350-unit public housing project. Next to the village was the 5,000-seat Palazzetto dello Sport. Designed by Annibale Vitellozzi and engineered by Pier Luigi Nervi, this domed concrete structure, glazed over a single storey base of red brick, was used for boxing and weight-lifting. Vitellozzi also designed the Stadio del Nuoto swimming and diving stadium, the last open-air pool used for an Olympic games.

The Olympic village, the Palazzetto and the 45,000-seat reinforced concrete Flaminio

soccer stadium – also engineered by Nervi and also open-air (although five gymnasiums and a swimming pool are tucked under its grandstand) – formed one group of buildings. A second was dominated by the 100,000-seat Stadio Olimpico, a huge colonnaded bowl fitted into an undulating site at the base of the Monte Mario hills, which formed an amphitheatre around it. The work of several architects, it was begun by Enrico del Debbio and finished by Vitellozzi in 1953. The infield of the stadium was set 5 metres (16 feet) below ground level and a deep trench separated it from the spectators.

The third building group was centred on the EUR precinct in the south of the city. This area had been set aside by Benito Mussolini for an international exposition scheduled for 1942 and abandoned as a result of World War Two. The Olympic contribution was the Palazzo dello Sport, an enlarged version of the Palazzetto designed by Pier Luigi Nervi and Marcello Piacentini. The column-free interior of this 16,000-seat hall was a feat of engineering, roofed with a 100-metre (330-foot) dome formed from 144 precast reinforced concrete rib sections.

Tokyo
1964

Whilst the Rome Olympics succeeded in assembling a dazzling collection of buildings that almost eclipsed the games themselves, it is true to say that not all of them were conceived for the games alone. The next Olympic games, the first ever to be held in Asia, showed how the task of creating an architectural setting could be taken to even greater extremes. In Tokyo in 1964 the world saw for the first time what could be done when the Olympic challenge was answered not so much by athletic performance as by a massive urban building programme designed to change forever the image of the city as well as that of the games.

In the early 1960s the Japanese economic miracle was approaching its apogee. Nothing seemed impossible, yet when the Japanese proposed spending $2 billion at 1960 values (approximately $22 billion today) on the Tokyo games, the International Olympic Committee openly doubted the feasibility of what they proposed. Their plan included purpose-made Olympic buildings and sports centres, as well as new parks, subway lines, hotels, commercial and residential buildings and, most radical of all, an 80-kilometre (50-mile) network of elevated expressways with 22 off-ramps to ease access to the Olympic site. One road alone, the elevated four-lane 'Olympic Highway' led directly from Haneda international airport to the Olympic Stadium in the outer gardens of the Meiji shrine, enabling the journey to be completed in 20 minutes instead of the hour previously required.

The Tokyo Olympic stadium itself had originally been built for the 1958 Asian Games but had been enlarged by the addition of a new seating tier for the Olympics, taking its capacity from 55,000 to 70,000. Also added were huge floodlighting masts so that, for the first time in the history of the games, events could be held after dark. But impressive though the upgraded stadium was, it lacked the impact of two smaller fully enclosed structures designed by Kenzo Tange and URTEC, with the help of engineers Yoshikatsu Tsuboi and Uichi Inoue. These were the 4,000-seat swimming arena and the 15,000-seat sports arena, built adjoining one another in the landscaped Yoyogi Sports Park. These two buildings, alike except in size – like the Palazzo and the Palazzetto in Rome – are widely considered to be the finest ensemble of Olympic buildings yet designed. In both arenas the seating galleries were developed as concrete arches cantilevered over rows of recessed columns. A search for the right means of enclosing these spaces led the architect Tange to tented forms: a ridge tent for the larger and a bell tent for the smaller. The long supporting catenary cables, stayed by massive ground anchors, look forward with uncanny precision to the work of Behnisch and Otto in Munich eight years later. On a third site, the former baseball ground at Komazawa, another sports complex was built, including a 22,000-seat open soccer stadium by Yutaka Murata, with fake 'monorail' VIP suites, and also a gymnasium by Yoshinobu Ashihara. All were overlooked by a 76-metre (249-foot) tree-like control tower that was a lineal descendant of the theatrical Helsinki tower of 1952.

Opposite: Interior of the main gym designed by Kenzo Tange for the Tokyo 1964 Olympics.

Mexico
1968

After the architectural riches and massive infrastructural spending of Tokyo, there was a return to fundamentalism in design in the Olympic movement that was perceptible in both the setting for the Mexico City games of 1968 and the Munich games of 1972. Mexico City boasted several stadiums, but the best known, the University Stadium, was originally built in 1953 with a capacity of 70,000 spectators and was enlarged to a capacity of 87,000 for the games. The University Stadium was fundamentalist in the sense that, like the unused Berlin stadium of 1913, it was basically an earth structure using very little concrete, exploiting the natural land slope to provide good sightlines. Much more prominent in an architectural sense was the covered Aztec Stadium by architect Pedro Ramirez Vasquez. With a capacity of 107,000 seated spectators, this is still considered to be the largest covered stadium in the world.

Opposite: Exterior view of the stadium for the 1972 Munich Olympics by Gunther Behnisch and Frei Otto.

Munich
1972

In 1972 the Olympics returned to Germany, to an abandoned airstrip on the western outskirts of the city of Munich where mounds of wartime rubble had been dumped. By skilful earth moving and landscaping this wasteland was converted into a 283-hectare (700-acre) park with hills, valleys, lakes and trees. The competition-winning Olympic buildings by Gunther Behnisch and Frei Otto were set among these artificial hills, the largest of them being the Olympic stadium, an elliptical pre-cast concrete structure seating 47,000 with provision for another 33,000 standing. Sheltering the stadium over more than half its area was the celebrated lightweight roof of transparent acrylic panels suspended from a steel tension net that was itself supported by a series of inclined masts held in place by ground anchors. This unique 8-hectare (21-acre) roof, which extends beyond the stadium to cover a sports hall and an Olympic pool, has not proved entirely trouble-free but it is now undergoing a rolling refurbishment programme. In addition to the main Olympic buildings, the Munich Olympic village was a considerable success. Designed by Heinle, Wischer and Associates and consisting of three snaking tiers of high-rise apartments interspersed with informal low-rise accommodation, it subsequently became a popular residential district.

As in Rome and Tokyo, the coming of the games brought changes to the city and the city brought changes to the games. On one level the Munich games is remembered for its 'new' architecture and for the first large-scale use of computers: on another it is remembered for the tragic slaughter of Israeli athletes by Arab terrorists, an event that not only colours all memories of the games to this day, but moved the issue of security on to the agenda for all future Olympics.

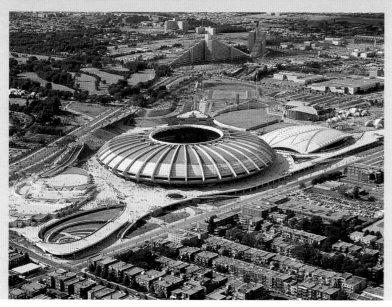

Montreal
1976

Up until 1976, apart from the earliest events linked to exhibitions, all modern Olympics had been paid for by state or city governments. As we have seen, the most expensive games ever was Tokyo in 1964, but even the Munich games cost an estimated $600 million, or nearer $3.6 billion at current values. Politicians had long voiced concern at rising Olympic costs, complaining that only the richest nations could afford to stage the games, but in Montreal, venue for the 1976 games, the mayor of the city, Jean Drapeau, was convinced that the games could be made to pay for themselves. His budget from public sector sources, established in 1972, was a pared down $310 million – $250 million for construction and the rest for organization. So sure was Drapeau that his games would not run a deficit that he pledged

the city of Montreal to repay the Canadian government if any should occur. Yet on 17 July 1976, when the Montreal Olympic games began, over $800 million had already been spent, and the main buildings were still incomplete.

The Montreal Olympic games were chiefly held on a vast concrete deck in a spectacular collection of expressionist concrete buildings comprising a covered 60,000-seat Olympic stadium (without its promised retractable fabric roof); an aquatic centre housed in the base of the unfinished tower intended to support the fabric roof; a separate 6,000-seat concrete velodrome; and two smaller arenas. The stadium itself was a tour de force of epoxy-bonded pre-cast concrete construction, its four tiers of seating supported by 34 massive elliptical concrete bents in 17 different sizes whose internal cantilevers soared out over the seating tiers to meet a compression ring 50 metres (164 feet) above the red cinder and grass infield. The absent cantilevered tower, which was to have held up the retractable fabric roof by means of radiating cables tied back to the ring beam,

was also to have contained administrative offices and been surmounted by a restaurant reached by an inclined lift. Although some of these elements were installed after the games, others have never been built or have never operated correctly, including the fabric roof. The same cannot be said of the satellite velodrome which, in the form of an upturned shield, spans an impressive 170 metres (557 feet) and admits a great quantity of daylight through acrylic blister rooflights. This building was completed, even though the construction of its roof was enormously complicated by the fact that 144 pre-cast subsections – no two the same size and all weighing between 50 and 100 tonnes – had

to be held in position while in-situ slabs were poured and then the entire 41,000 tonne assembly was raised on jacks in order to remove the scaffolding. Like the aquatic centre buried in the base of the uncompleted tower, the velodrome is considered by some to have been among the best Olympic structures ever built.

All these epic Montreal buildings were designed by the Paris architect Roger Taillibert who was commissioned directly by Mayor Drapeau without the formality of an architectural competition, a matter that caused considerable controversy after the games when the post-mortem began in earnest. In the months and years that followed it became clear that the stadium had cost $800 million instead of an estimated $132 million, and the velodrome $86 million instead of $20 million. The final cost of the 'self-financing' Montreal Olympic Park was in excess of $6 billion at current values, a debt which the city is still paying off.

Moscow
1980

Barcelona
1992

While the scandal of the cost excesses at Montreal must have seemed to the Soviet organizers of the 1980 Olympics to be a textbook example of the inherent contradictions of capitalism bringing about its own destruction, problems of a different order were to confront Moscow in due course. The Soviets had announced a budget of $375 million – much less than the out-turn at Montreal – and added the cost of new buildings for the Olympics to the budget for the nation's tenth Five Year Plan. Making use of existing sports facilities like the giant oval 100,000-seat Lenin Stadium in Moscow, completed in 1956 to designs by Wlassov, Polikarpov and Resnikov, may have saved money for the first socialist Olympics, but it hardly made up for the United States-led boycott brought about by the collision of Soviet and United States foreign policy in Afghanistan. This led to the absence of Americans, Canadians, West Germans, Japanese and athletes from many smaller nations. Nor did it compensate for the cost of 90 construction sites in the Soviet Union and Estonia where Olympics-related facilities were built. The fact that the boycott was played in reverse four years later when Los Angeles hosted the 1984 Olympics – and the way in which the rising issue of security marred the use of the dry moat-surrounded 100,000-seat Seoul stadium of 1988, serves only to underline the political platform that the games had become during the later Cold War years.

The first post-Cold War Olympics took place in the Spanish city of Barcelona. There the once overwhelming trend in favour of new construction was reversed yet again as elements of the older Olympic tradition of refurbishment and reuse came to the fore. Starting with the stadium built for the 1929 World's Fair on the neglected Montjuic site, the Olympic competition-winning architect Vittorio Gregotti gutted its interior, leaving only the Romanesque façade intact. Once everything inside the perimeter walls had been removed, the infield was lowered in order to double the previous seating capacity to 80,000. At the same time, a new tunnel system was installed beneath the 9-lane running track so that officials and the media could circulate freely around the stadium without interfering with events. The stadium was then used to accommodate virtually all the track and field sports on the Olympic programme. Outside the main gate of the stadium, a new piazza was laid down from which access could be gained to four other buildings: the 17,000-seat Palau Sant Jordi gymnasium by Arata Isozaki; the Picornell swimming complex; the university of sport and an international media centre. The tight composition of this assembly of buildings meant that the Barcelona Olympic site was considerably smaller than all those occupied by previous post-war games except the Olympic Park at Montreal.

Following pages: The Palau Sant Jordi gymnasium by Arata Isozaki for the 1992 Olympic games in Barcelona.

Atlanta
1996

In the end the thorny issue of rising costs and the mirage of the 'self-financing games' were overcome only through the merging of amateur and professional sport – in effect the total commodification of the Olympic building process – that took place in 1996 in Atlanta. There, a consortium of designers called the ASDT (Atlanta Stadium Design Team) led by architects Ellerbe Becket contrived to create an 85,000-seat arena in a watered down postmodern style that would conform to the tone and bulk of the buildings within an 'Olympic Ring' close to the centre of the city. The main feature of the stadium in technical terms was the provision that it should be cut in half to leave a 48,000-seat baseball park for the Atlanta Braves after the games were over. The 100,000 square metre (1,000,000 square foot)

composite steel and concrete stadium was designed for optimum performance in both its roles. Sightlines, circulation and access, food services and media requirements, as well as special seating for Olympic officials and luxury suites for baseball games, were all fitted into the asymmetrical three-tier seating arrangement, part of which has now given place to office space and a public park.

The Atlanta Olympic games took place against the background of a new sports building boom in the United States. Indeed it formed part of it. This boom followed the rediscovery of the advantages of the downtown sports stadium after 50 years of emphasis on the suburbs and the exploitation of its new role as a catalyst for urban renewal. The subsequent realization of the commercial potential of these new structures as total sports, entertainment, retail and media experiences has brought forth a whole new level of investment and design ingenuity. Today, American stadium design, unfettered by the four-yearly Olympic timetable, but borrowing from its successes, combines the entertainment environment of

the Universal Studios tour with the spectator experience of a perfectly designed arena. As a result of the success of the genre there now exists a tremendous concentration of sports/entertainment architectural expertise in the United States.

Ellerbe Becket's own follow-up to the Atlanta Olympic stadium is a case in point. After designing a stadium for the unsuccessful Manchester bid for the Olympics of 2000 – now awarded to Sydney – the firm went to work on a giant arena for the Diamond Backs professional baseball team. Called 'Bank One Ballpark' – because the eponymous Phoenix-based bank paid $30 million for the right to name it – this stadium in Phoenix, Arizona, opened in 1998. A 48,000-seat, triple tier arena occupying six city blocks and towering above the city's predominantly low-rise

architecture, this huge building surrounds its 16,000 square metre (172,000 square foot) ballpark with 10,000 square metres (107,600 square feet) of entertainment and merchandising floor space tucked in beneath its grandstands – all accessible from the street as well as from inside the arena. There could be no contrast as powerful as the difference between this structure, driven by its retail and entertainment facilities, and the stark beauty of the World Cup stadium at Bari, in Italy, designed by Renzo Piano ten years before.

The Bank One Ballpark effortlessly overcomes the operating constraints imposed by Phoenix's harsh desert climate. Its stadium is not only air-conditioned but has a fully retractable sliding roof, permitting the use of natural turf and allowing games to be played day or night during the hottest and coldest months. Like the earlier roof-opening Toronto Skydome of 1989, the sheer scale of this structure in relation to the rest of the city is hard to comprehend. Bank One's roof is so enormous that each side-supporting rail is 150 metres long (492 feet) – nearly the length of two soccer pitches.

Oblique aerial view plus CAD image of the finished Sydney 2000 Olympic park at Homebush Bay.

Of this mighty construction, Ellerbe Becket director William Johnson has said, 'Stadiums of this size can be understood at different levels. In one sense they are simply giant cash registers, backdrops for the merchandising of sports celebrities. In another they are the definitive structures of our time, as much as the great cathedrals were the definitive structures of the middle ages.'

Ethics and aggression may be the heads and tails of winning, as anthropologist Robert Ardrey suggested 30 years ago. But he wrote at a time when the media and retail frenzy accompanying all major sporting events today barely existed. Perhaps the final judgement on the role of Olympic architecture in the twentieth century should turn his insight into a question: 'If ethics and aggression are the heads and tails of sport, is design alone what keeps them apart?' For if it is, does not the merging of the Olympic ideal with commercial sports architecture – the combination so successful in Atlanta in 1996 and anticipated for Sydney in 2000 – present us with that fusion of the sacred and profane that Baron Pierre de Coubertin sought to prevent?

6

The Rules of the Game

Richard Williams

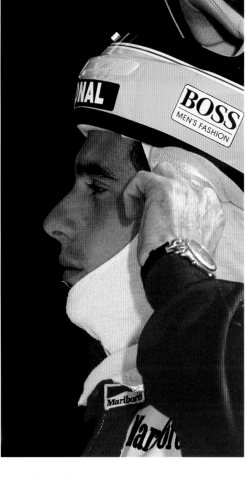

Opposite: Driving a Mercedes, Stirling Moss was the first British driver to win the British Grand Prix at Aintree in 1955. Above: Ayrton Senna removing his bright yellow signature helmet.

Sport doesn't change much, the wisdom goes. The Oxford–Cambridge Boat Race is still just a giant game of Pooh sticks, its essential simplicity equally unaffected by the advent of sponsorship or the use of computer-designed carbon-fibre boats instead of the lovely clinker-built wooden shells of the olden days. The men's 100-metre race at the Olympic games is changed neither by the fact that the runners are wearing aerodynamic one-piece suits in a low-resistance synthetic fabric, nor by the knowledge that the winner will become a millionaire in little more than the time he takes to cover the course. And, like the cockroach, the noble art of boxing survives from time immemorial into a new millennium, as if to remind us of our barbarbic past and of our unreconstructed nature.

It's a comforting theory. Whatever might happen in the wider world, it says, man's urge to compete and conquer is primeval and inalterable. Essentially, Jack Johnson and Mike Tyson are the same man: they hit, they hurt. There is no difference between Jesse Owens, black star of the Berlin Olympics in 1936, and Donovan Bailey, the winner of the gold medal for the men's sprint at the 1996 Atlanta Games. The film *A Yank At Oxford* could be remade on the Isis today without much need for a script rewrite.

And it's true, up to a point. The boats and the running shoes are made of more helpful high-technology materials, while the training methods and the medical support have improved a hundredfold, but success in these basic sports comes down, in the end, to the same basic qualities: the conversion of physical strength into power, driven by tightly focused self-belief. In the end, the athlete with the best grip on these faculties will triumph.

But one of the best things about sport is the fact that different games require different combinations of attributes. And, naturally, many of the games invented during the twentieth century have taken advantage of their contemporary nature to indulge in rapid evolution of technology and technique. Some sports have done this in a minor way. In football, for instance, changes to the surface material, the weight, and the internal pressure of the ball itself have combined with new features in footwear manufacture to give such players as Alessandro del Piero, of Juventus and Italy, and Roberto Carlos, of Real Madrid and Brazil, the opportunity to strike their free kicks with a hitherto unknown combination of pace and swerve. Improvements in metallurgy and ballistics have allowed javelin throwers to set new records in recent years – although some of these improvements have proved too much for the sport's governing body. When the World Athletics Championships were held in Tokyo in 1991, the provision of an advanced rubber-based track with high-rebound characteristics ensured that several new world records were set by the sprinters, who found the power in their legs enhanced by the bounce of the track.

Hinged ice skates, known as 'klapp' skates because of the noise they make, have recently appeared in speed skating, contributing to large increases in performance. The titanium shaft and oversized head of his driver has helped Tiger Woods to hit a golf ball further, therefore bringing the putting greens within easier reach and improving his chances of a low score, although the advantage is reduced by the fact that the same implement is available to his fellow competitors.

But these modifications changed only the detail of each sport, not its inherent characteristics. Among those disciplines that have experienced significant change in recent years as a direct result of technological development, no example is more spectacular or instructive than that of Formula One motor racing, the annual 16-race world championship Grand Prix series, which is now, according to its impresarios, the world's second most widely watched television sport, after football, with aggregate viewing figures over a season numbered in the tens of billions. By dedicating itself to wooing television networks and their audiences, Formula One has provided an object lesson in how equipment technology and the mass media can broaden the appeal of a sport, while almost completely changing its nature.

After World War Two, motor racing was slow to pick up its pieces. But when it re-emerged, with the birth of the world championship series in 1950, it was still a reflection of what it had been in earlier times – an élite sport, the pursuit of rich amateurs and wealthy industrialists. Few of the world's major motor manufacturers took part. Those racing firms that did sell road cars were usually small specialists, such as Ferrari, Bugatti and Maserati. With the growth of British participation in Formula One came the dominance of companies that didn't make road cars at all – Vanwall, BRM, Cooper, McLaren, Williams. The reappearance of major manufacturers in the 1980s, as suppliers of engines to the specialist chassis-builders, allowed firms such as Honda, Renault, Mercedes-Benz and Peugeot to share in the glory of competitive success without accepting the full risk of technical failure.

But they were returning, many of them, to a world that had cunningly recreated itself as a worldwide franchise, as a remarkably efficient vehicle for global advertising campaigns (and, in the case of tobacco companies, for advertising that could find few other legitimate outlets). Best of all, they were involved in a sport that had found a way of reconstructing itself as, in effect, a running news story, with soap-opera overtones which gave it regular access to large amounts of newsprint and airtime. And for this, new technology was largely responsible.

In the immediate post-war years, during the era dominated by Juan Manuel Fangio, the five-times world champion, and Stirling Moss, his uncrowned heir, the sport adhered very largely to the moral codes laid down by earlier generations. Fatal accidents were common in motor racing then, and the drivers would do nothing that might increase the likelihood of such tragedies, or indeed put their rivals at any sort of risk. The exceptions – such as the first post-war world champion, Dr Nino Farina, who was not averse to nudging opponents out of the way – were regarded with disapproval, but such was the code of honour that their behaviour was tolerated as an aberration, and remained unexposed.

The principal reason for the observance of ethical duelling standards was the knowledge that the cars were lethal enough, without the sport being made even more dangerous by the behaviour of the men who drove them. Built as light as possible to improve the vital ratio of engine power to overall weight, the cars were for many years little more than mobile bombs – the driver sat in an aluminium cocoon surrounded by highly frangible tanks carrying large amounts of high-octane fuel. And the drivers were afforded virtually no protection at all by their own personal kit – helmets made of thin layers of leather and cork, plain cotton overalls, ordinary underwear and string-backed gloves with no flameproofing, and no safety harnesses. The circuits were mostly laid out over public roads, sustaining a link with the earliest days of the sport, when the cars and drivers raced from city to city, but also maintaining a great variety of natural hazards. Death by fire, or death by impact with stone walls or unprotected trees and telegraph poles, accounted for the disappearance of dozens of drivers in the 1950s and 1960s, including such famous names as Alberto Ascari, Peter Collins, Eugenio Castellotti, Jean Behra, Lorenzo Bandini and Jochen Rindt.

The deaths of Rindt, his best friend, and Francois Cevert, his team-mate, impelled

Top: Juan Manuel Fangio behind the wheel of the Alfetta 159 Alfa Romeo in which he won the 1951 World Championship. Above: Jackie Stewart in a Matra Ford in 1963. Opposite: Each Formula One car is a collection of over 3,000 parts, mostly computer-designed and manufactured in-house. Following pages: Jacques Villeneuve storms into the lead at the 1997 British Grand Prix at Silverstone. While sponsorship has always been a key element in American racing, teams racing in Europe before 1968 were required to run cars in traditional national colours: British racing green, Italian red, German silver, French blue.

Opposite: Ayrton Senna at the 1993 Monaco Grand Prix. It was his tactics that turned Formula One into a contact sport and gave rise to a new code of driving conduct. Above: David Coulthard and Michael Schumacher clash during the 1998 Argentinian Grand Prix. The development of fat racing tyres rendered the cars considerably safer.

Jackie Stewart to lead a crusade for greater awareness of safety precautions. Unburstable petrol tanks were borrowed from the aircraft industry, as were elaborate safety harnesses and crash helmets that offered all-round protection. Ambulances, trained safety crews and fully equipped fire marshals' posts were introduced. And when Niki Lauda almost died in the conflagration after his Ferrari hit an earth bank in the far reaches of the 14-mile Nurburgring circuit in Germany's Eiffel mountains, the circuits themselves came under scrutiny. No more telegraph poles, trees, concrete walls, earth banks or straw bales. No more tramlines, which had been a feature of a street circuit like Oporto in Portugal. No more high kerbs, such as had lined the roads around Monaco. No more 14-mile circuits, indeed, since they could not be adequately staffed. And, less obviously but just as crucially, no more wacky, way-out car designs, united only by a common engine size. The parameters of the new regulations laid down the permissible maxima of height, length, width, and many other dimensions which future generations of car designers would have to observe.

Instituted largely for reasons of cost and through a desire to maintain a rough equality of competition, these measures also served to

cut down the risk of a maverick designer building a physically unsound, and therefore dangerous, car. Coincidentally, the development of fat racing tyres rendered the cars considerably safer: with a great energy-absorbent gumball at each corner of the chassis, they were less likely to be damaged by minor collisions on a crowded track.

For the first time since the dawn of the century, when men raced from Paris to Lyon on unmetalled roads in cars whose solid rubber tyres were steered by tillers, safety became a factor. As the carnage of two world wars receded in the collective memory, and the Battle of Britain ethos was relegated to black and white movies, so the idea of putting a value on a human life entered the most fatally dangerous of sports.

And yet, curiously, the safety precautions were the very factors that finally undermined the old etiquette of racing – the chivalry, the unselfishness, the sense of honour. Once the drivers became virtually invulnerable, once it was established that they could now survive 180 mph impacts, cartwheels and somersaults, and that even a flash fire could be extinguished in a matter of seconds by a combination of onboard fuel cutoff devices and efficient marshalling, they were licensed to behave towards each other with a brutality that sometimes verged on the thuggish.

It took them a while to wake up to the new reality. When Gilles Villeneuve and Rene Arnoux banged the wheels of their Ferrari and Renault all the way round the final lap of the French Grand Prix in the early 1980s, neither man giving way and both finishing the race with smiles on their faces, most commentators thought it was marvellous fun, very spectacular, a grand exhibition of sporting daredevilry. And, thanks to the strong construction of their cars and the special properties of their fat tyres, they could get away with it. Later in the decade, however, the mood surrounding such tactics changed entirely, thanks to the rivalry between two men, Alain Prost and Ayrton Senna.

Since his death in an unexplained crash at the Imola track in 1994, Senna has become a figure practically beyond reproach. But it is a fact that his tactics, often employed to gain the upper hand over Prost, turned Formula One into the one thing it never was: a contact sport.

During the years of his apprenticeship, Senna developed a method of intimidating his rivals through a combination of brilliant talent and sheer physical ruthlessness. He wore a bright yellow helmet, inside which burnt a self-belief perhaps unmatched in any sport at any time. When another driver saw that helmet coming up behind him, wanting to get by, he knew he had to give Senna room or risk the consequences. 'He left it up to you whether you wanted to have an accident with him or not,' was how one of his contemporaries and early rivals, Martin Brundle, put it. In the smaller cars of the lesser formulae, running at lower speeds, these accidents rarely had serious consequences. But when Senna graduated to Formula One, he took his techniques with him – and began to exercise them on the senior drivers. It worked, because he was so talented. Had he ever felt in need of an excuse, he might plausibly have pointed out that the nature of the cars, so similar in performance that the drivers were finding it almost impossible to overtake each other, made it difficult for him to express that talent. And since he believed his talent was given by God, to deny it was to frustrate the divine will.

How Senna would have got on in the 1930s, when the cars ran on spindly tyres and would overturn at the slightest nudge, or in the 1950s, when the drivers had alloy petrol tanks packed around their thighs and sometimes over their knees, is an interesting question. But the technology of his era allowed him to change the rules of the game, to such influential effect that his successor, Michael Schumacher, turned what Senna had done by instinct into a system of victory. Like Senna, Schumacher could invoke a wonderfully paradoxical self-justification: being unquestionably the most talented driver in the field, he could claim a moral right to win by any means necessary, since victory, however achieved, would only confirm the correct order of things.

The further consequence of these cold-blooded hand-to-hand battles – Senna versus Prost or Nigel Mansell, Schumacher versus Damon Hill or Jacques Villeneuve – was a raising of the sport's profile among a different audience. Suddenly the tabloid newspapers loved Formula One, and gave its feuding heroes vast amounts of space on their sports pages, encouraging them to extend the competition into wars of recriminatory words. As long as this level of personal antagonism could be sustained, so Formula One would retain its box-office appeal, and continue to make millionaires of many of its principal actors and supporting cast. And all of it, all this overhyped publicity and phenomenal financial prosperity, was enabled by the development of the sport's technology.

Grand Prix racing is an extreme example. Top-level motorcycle racing, by contrast, has not benefitted in the same way because motorbike riders cannot be made as safe inside their vehicles as Formula One drivers. But in other sports, other forms of protection have changed the way the games are played. Rugby Union players, for example, have experienced a similar phenomenon since body armour – chest and shoulder protection, copied from American football – came into widespread use. This padding allows players to give and take bigger, more spectacular 'hits', which have swiftly become an even more significant part of an already macho game. And, in a distantly related evolutionary line, slalom skiers can take straighter lines through their gates, thanks to reinforced helmets, gloves and shin-guards, and to special hinges that allow racers to slap the slalom poles aside as they pass.

There is one obvious conclusion. In a world that seems to be growing ever more conscious of the sanctity of human life, and is less inclined to encourage people to take risks with their mortality, we look to sport to give us the sensation of danger. But only the sensation. Not the reality. And thanks to the invention of the autoclaves in which carbon-fibre is baked, and thanks to the development of lightweight Kevlar body armour and flame-resistant cloth, the long-anticipated era of Rollerball is, for better or worse, just about here.

Above: Even with today's technology, competition motorcycle riders cannot be made as safe as Formula One drivers. Opposite: Design has changed the way sports are played. Reinforced clothing and the special hinges on the poles allow the slalom skier to take straighter lines through the gates.

Bibliography

Ardrey, Robert, *The Territorial Imperative*, Collins, London 1967

Burgoyne, Patrick and Jeremy Leslie, *Bored: Surf/Skate/Snow Graphics*, Laurence King, London 1997

Burgoyne, Patrick and Jeremy Leslie, *FC Football Graphics*, Thames & Hudson, London 1998

Busch, Akiko (ed.), *Design for Sport: The Cult of Performance*, Cooper-Hewitt National Design Museum, Smithsonian Institution/Thames & Hudson, London 1998

Coleman, Nick and Nick Hornby (eds), *The Picador Book of Sports Writing*, Picador, London 1996

Design Museum, *Sport 90*, London 1990

Furedi, Frank, *Culture of Fear, Risk-Taking and the Morality of Low Expectation*, Cassell, London 1997

Gordon, Barclay, *Olympic Architecture: Building for the Summer Games*, Wiley Interscience, New York 1983

Hornby, Nick, *Fever Pitch: A Fan's Life*, Victor Gollancz, London 1992

Jarvie, Grant and Joseph Maguire, *Sport and Leisure in Social Thought*, Routledge, London 1994

John, Geraint and Rod Sheard, *Stadia: A Design and Development Guide*, Architectural Press, Oxford 1998

Polley, Martin, *Moving the Goalposts: A History of Sport and Society since 1945*, Routledge, London 1998

Raitz, Karl B. (ed.), *The Theater of Sport*, Johns Hopkins University Press, Baltimore 1995

Roche, Maurice (ed.), *Sport, Popular Culture and Identity*, Meyer & Meyer Verlag, Aachen 1998

Walpole, Brenda, *Science of Sport*, Trustees of the Science Museum, London 1997

Williams, Richard, *The Death of Ayrton Senna*, Penguin, London 1995

Williams, Richard, *Racers*, Penguin, London 1998

Credits

Index